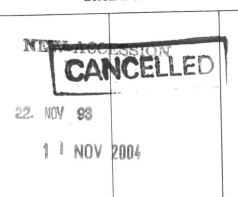

The Rabbit

The Rabbit A Model for the Principles of Mammalian Physiology and Surgery

HAROLD M. KAPLAN

School of Medicine
Southern Illinois University at Carbondale
Carbondale, Illinois

EDWARD H. TIMMONS

Albert B. Chandler Medical Center
Division of Animal Care Services
University of Kentucky
Lexington, Kentucky

ACADEMIC PRESS

New York   San Francisco   London   1979
A Subsidiary of Harcourt Brace Jovanovich, Publishers

COPYRIGHT © 1979, BY ACADEMIC PRESS, INC.
ALL RIGHTS RESERVED.
NO PART OF THIS PUBLICATION MAY BE REPRODUCED OR
TRANSMITTED IN ANY FORM OR BY ANY MEANS, ELECTRONIC
OR MECHANICAL, INCLUDING PHOTOCOPY, RECORDING, OR ANY
INFORMATION STORAGE AND RETRIEVAL SYSTEM, WITHOUT
PERMISSION IN WRITING FROM THE PUBLISHER.

ACADEMIC PRESS, INC.
111 Fifth Avenue, New York, New York 10003

United Kingdom Edition published by
ACADEMIC PRESS, INC. (LONDON) LTD.
24/28 Oval Road, London NW1   7DX

Library of Congress Cataloging in Publication Data

Kaplan, Harold Morris, Date
  The rabbit.

  Bibliography: p.
  1. Surgery, Experimental. 2. Physiology, Experimental. 3. Rabbits as laboratory animals.
4. Rabbits——Surgery. 5. Rabbits——Physiology.
I. Timmons, Edward H., joint author. II. Title.
RD29.5.R33K36   636.089'7   78–67878
ISBN 0–12–397450–X

PRINTED IN THE UNITED STATES OF AMERICA

79 80 81 82   9 8 7 6 5 4 3 2 1

Contents

Chapter 3
Principles and Applications of Rabbit Anesthesia

PART II

Laboratory Procedures Using the Rabbit

Chapter 4
General Mammalian Physiology and Surgical Techniques

Contents

Chapter 5

Advanced Specialized Procedures

Preface

This text has three distinct goals and audiences in mind. The first goal is the training of students in experimental animal surgery. The second is the presentation of a broad spectrum of exercises to satisfy the needs of students and courses in mammalian physiology. These two goals are almost inseparably linked with regard to the kinds of students involved and the selection of material relevant to both groups. The third goal is the presentation of selected advanced procedures that are of interest to professional investigators, whether in academic institutions, pharmaceutical houses, or other places where animal experimentation is being conducted.

The high cost of cats and dogs, the problems involved in their proper handling and care, and the unfavorable position of collegiate programs in obtaining them makes it advisable to seek less controversial animals to illustrate physiologic principles. This has already been successfully done with rats. The rabbit lends itself perhaps even more readily to certain kinds of experimentation. It is easily housed and handled, and it is sufficiently hardy to be an animal of choice for exercises at the senior college and graduate level, particularly if the exercises are properly supervised and if they are presented in a sequence that allows the student to learn the manipulative procedures with increasing facility.

The procedures selected for discussion can be successfully accomplished by students working in teams. Most of the exercises require at least two hours for their orderly accomplishment. Some of them are designed for the student who needs to develop proficiency in laboratory animal surgery. Other exercises meet the needs of a generalized course in mammalian physiology. The selection of work should satisfy either goal. The majority of the exercises involve acute terminal experimentation. The chronic surgical work should give the student the knowledge and responsibility of caring for his animals over a short period of time. The exercises favor a division of responsibility among teams, each team and its members having selected tasks in a given project.

To obtain individual proficiency, we recommend rotation of tasks, such as surgeon and anesthetist, in the surgical exercises. Also, we recommend that many surgical exercises be repeated. The written procedures should be continually altered to suit the kinds of equipment that become available in the field.

Exercises that are representative of the field have been selected for the student work. Several of them have been adapted from the original research literature, with the conviction that the creative thinking of the past, as well as of the present, is a stimulating source for the teaching of students. For this reason, the original literature is also frequently cited.

The rabbit is coming into increasing prominence as a favored animal for training and for research in the biologic sciences. The student must be taught, however, that the use of live animals is a hard-won privilege. Whatever opportunities we now possess could be removed by failure to treat every animal as humanely as possible. The profession has the duty to police itself through proper education. In using a single species, the student can become increasingly familiar with its habits, needs, and signs of discomfort and disease; and can also reach a decision as to whether some simpler form of life could just as readily serve for a particular kind of experimentation.

The "junior" surgery and general mammalian aspect of this text can easily be adapted to either quarter or semester systems. We run courses for two semesters of seventeen weeks each. The first semester is didactic. There is class discussion of such topics as anesthetics, sterilization, infection and immunity, the repair of wounds, drug actions and dosages, and other topics in the province of pathology, pharmacology, and surgery. The second semester is devoted to exercises that emphasize surgery of one laboratory species and to selected exercises covering a broad spectrum of mammalian physiology.

We are particularly indebted to Ms. Janice K. Kuse and Mrs. Catherine A. Mabus at Southern Illinois University for their painstaking assistance not only in a clerical sense but also in regard to their valuable editorial suggestions. Illustrations were done by Ms. Karen Schmitt and the photography by John A. Richardson. Additionally, the feedback from a generation of students who have tested the validity of the exercises has an enduring value.

Harold M. Kaplan
Edward H. Timmons

The Rabbit

Part *I* Rabbit Data and General Surgical Principles

Chapter *1* Rabbit Data and Essential Procedures

A. PRINCIPLES OF LABORATORY ANIMAL CARE

The following principles, quoted in full, were developed by the cooperative effort of the American Association of Laboratory Animal Science, the National Academy of Sciences and the National Society for Medical Research:

1. All animals used for experimental purposes must be lawfully acquired. Standards for their care shall be in strict compliance with federal, state, and local laws, and with pertinent government and institutional regulations

2. Scientific institutions shall maintain a standing committee, or other appropriate administrative body to set policies and guidelines for the use and care of animals in experiments conducted under their auspices. These policies and guidelines shall be in accordance with the recommendations of the Institute for Laboratory Animal Resources (NAS-NRC).

3. Experiments involving live animals must be performed by, or under the immediate supervision of, a qualified biological scientist.

4. The housing, care, and feeding of all experimental animals shall be supervised by a properly qualified veterinarian or other biological scientist competent in such matters.

5. All laboratory animals must receive every consideration for their comfort; they must be kindly treated, properly fed, and their surroundings kept in a sanitary condition.

6. In any operation likely to cause greater discomfort than that attending anesthetization, the animal shall first be incapable of perceiving pain and be maintained in that condition until the operation is ended, except that whenever anesthetization would defeat the purpose of the experiment, the experiment must be specifically approved and supervised by the principal investigator in accordance with procedures established by the institutional committee.

   a. If an acute study does not require survival, the animal must be killed in a humane manner at the conclusion of the experiment by a procedure that insures immediate death, in accordance with practices established by the institutional committee. The animal is not to be discarded until its death is certain.

b. If the nature of the study is such as to require survival of the animals, acceptable techniques established by the institutional committee must be followed.

c. The postoperative care of animals must be such as to minimize discomfort during convalescence, in accordance with acceptable practices in veterinary medicine.

These principles as supplemented by institutional policy must be applied before any animal can be used for research purposes. The United States Federal Laws that currently relate to animal manipulation are P.L. 89–544 as amended by the Animal Welfare Act of 1970 (P.L. 91–579). The surgical team should also be familiar with the United States Department of Health, Education, and Welfare Publication "Guide for the Care and Use of Laboratory Animals."

B. BREEDS AND BREEDING

1. Useful Laboratory Breeds

Genetic uniformity is unnecessary in the kinds of work performed in our exercises so that the choice of strain is not a problem. The breed, however, is of importance. We have been able to use successfully the New Zealand white rabbit (*Oryctolagus cuniculus*) for diverse kinds of experimentation. As an albino, its ear veins are readily located for bleeding or injection. The young animal at 2½ to 3 kg body weight can provide a copious source of blood and it withstands general anesthesia and major surgery. It is readily manageable and its behavior predictable. Also, it is available from licensed breeders at all times of the year. It is resistant to disease when held under appropriate sanitary conditions and, following proper conditioning, it is an unlikely vector of disease to man. We recommend that one breed be used as much as possible so that the student can become thoroughly familiar with the characteristic responses of such animals. White rabbits much larger or much smaller than 2½ kg are not desirable except for specialized studies.

The American Rabbit Breeders Association lists 28 breeds and almost 80 varieties. Detailed information about the origin of inbred strains, nomenclature of strains and gene mutations, breeding systems, and genetics is available in "The Biology of the Laboratory Rabbit," prepared by the American College of Laboratory Animal Medicine, and published by Academic Press (Weisbroth *et al.*, 1974).

2. Data Concerning Growth and Reproduction

The life-span of rabbits is from 5 to 8 years. Large hybrids may live to 15 years. The indexes of age are not sharply defined and are variable with the breed. One index is the size and appearance of the claws. They do not project beyond the fur until the rabbit approaches maturity. The claws grow and curl with age. The ears of old rabbits are tougher to the touch than those of young animals.

We find that the albino rabbit weighing 2½ to 3 kg is satisfactory for most surgical procedures. The New Zealand white grows very rapidly and may weigh 1.8 kg as early as 8 weeks of age. The adults are in the range of 4 to 6 kg.

A rabbit of medium-sized breed reaches 2.3 kg at about 18 weeks, although this varies with many factors. Upon attaining a weight of 2.3 kg, it may take 6 weeks or more to gain an additional 0.5 kg.

The following growth table is cited from Altman and Dittmer (1972).

Weeks	Male (kg)	Female (kg)
18	2.8–3.7	2.9–4.0
20	2.8–3.9	3.0–4.3
22	3.0–4.0	3.3–4.4
24	3.0–4.3	3.4–4.8
26	3.0–4.4	3.5–4.9

The age of sexual maturity varies with the breed. The small breeds (Polish) are fertile at about 4 months, the medium breeds (New Zealand) at about 7 months, and the large breeds (Flemish) at 9 to 12 months. The following table summarizes relevant reproductive data for breeds of laboratory interest.

Gestation period	Average is 31 days (range is 30–35 days).
Type of estrous cycle	Continous.
Duration of heat (estrus) period	Ovulates 10 to 13 hours after copulation (Doe is brought to buck's hutch. Copulation is usually immediate. Doe is returned to its own cage).
Minimum breeding age	Up to 7 months, depending on breed.
Breeding season	All year (conception rate varies with seasonal temperature).
Average litter size	6 to 8, depending on breed.
Birth weight	100 gm, depending on breed.
Weaned	6 to 8 weeks (weight varies from 800 to 1500 gm).
Optimal breeding life	
Female	1 to 3 years.
Male	1 to 3 years.

cont'd

Cont'd

| Breeding method | 1 male to 1 female (1 male can service 6 to 10 females). |
| Rebreeding time after parturition | 35 days |

3. Breeding.   Breeding rabbits is not essential since clean stock is readily available from dependable licensed suppliers. Proper breeding in the laboratory, however, gives assurance that the offspring will be of the type demanded. *Inbreeding* can fix the type, but there are financial problems in discarding undesired forms. *Line breeding* is the same in principle, but the animals mated are not so closely related. *Cross-breeding* involves mating a purebred rabbit of one breed with a purebred rabbit of another.

The present account does not emphasize breeding since detailed information is available in the literature to the interested worker. Our interest is in those factors of reproduction of the rabbit which enter into the success of anesthesia and surgery and which need to be known in certain exercises.

C. PHYSIOLOGIC AND BIOCHEMICAL DATA FOR RABBITS

Several exercises herein involve changes in physiologic and biochemical data following manipulation or surgery. Accordingly, a table of normal data is presented. These data are highly variable, because of operator and instrumental errors and also because the data are dependent on animal variation, particularly age, breed, and sex.

Red blood cell count ($\times$ 10^6/mm³	6.26 to 6.30	HCO_3 concentration (mM/liter)	17
		PCO_2 (torr)	20 to 46
Red blood cell diameter (mμ)	6.5 to 7.5	Serum sodium (mEq/liter)	140
Red blood cell volume (μ^3)	60 to 68	Serum chloride (mEq/liter)	105
Packed cell volume (%)	40	Serum potassium (mEq/liter)	5 to 7
White blood cell count ($\times$ 10³/mm³)		Serum calcium (mg%)	9 to 12
Segmented neutrophils (%)	30 to 50	Serum phosphorus (mg%)	5 to 6
Eosinophils	0.5 to 5	Serum magnesium (mg%)	2.7
Monocytes	2 to 16	Serum iron (mg%)	130 to 210
Lymphocytes	30 to 50	Serum copper (mg%)	0.7 to 1.1
Basophils	2 to 8	Serum glucose (mg%)	80 to 110
Thrombocytes (platelets) ($\times$ 10³/mm³)		Serum total cholesterol (mg%)	50 to 100
	to 1,000	Blood urea nitrogen (BUN) (mg%)	5 to 20
Hemoglobin (gm/100 ml)	12.9 to 13.4	Serum protein (gm%)	7.2
Clotting time (with glass) (min)	5	Albumin (gm%)	4.6
Blood pH	7.35	Globulin (gm%)	2.7

cont'd

Cont'd

Total blood volume (ml/kg)	57.7 to 70	Serum total lipids (mg%)	325
Total body water (ml/kg)	668 to 743	Adult metabolism (cal/kg/day)	110
Osmotic fragility of red blood cells	0.3 to 0.5	Urine excreted daily (ml)	40 to 100
(in terms of percent of saline)		Feces excreted daily (gm)	15 to 60
Mean blood pressure in carotid artery (torr)		Daily food consumption of adult (gm)	
	90 to 100		150 to 200
Blood pressure (systolic-diastolic) (torr)		Daily water consumption of adult (ml)	300
	120/80	Renal clearance of inulin (ml/min/kg)	7.0
Heart rate (per min)	180		
Respiratory rate (per min in an animal not			
being handled)	50(32 to 60)		
Body temperature, rectal (°C)	39.4		
Tidal volume (ml)	21		
Total CO_2 concentration (mM/liter)	11 to 25		

D. ESSENTIAL PROCEDURES

1. Handling and Restraint

Proper rabbit handling is a necessity to prevent both animal and human injuries. A frightened rabbit which is not securely held has a tendency to kick violently with its rear legs, which can cause back injuries to the rabbit and scratches to the handler. A rabbit should be picked up by firmly, holding the loose skin over the scruff of the neck with one hand while supporting the rear legs with the other hand (Fig. 1). It is also acceptable to hold a rabbit by supporting its body with one arm while holding the scruff with the other hand (Fig. 2). Transporting rabbits to laboratories should be done in specially designed transport cages. The box-type cage should have a solid bottom to collect feces and

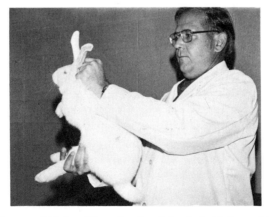

Figure 1. Proper rabbit handling. One hand firmly holds loose skin over scruff of the neck while other hand supports rear legs.

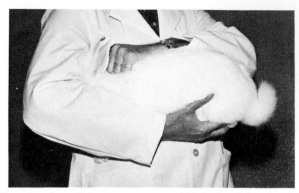

Figure 2.   Carrying the rabbit. Arm supports rabbit body while other hand holds neck scruff securely.

urine and the upper portion should be well ventilated. It should be constructed of a material that can withstand sanitizing or cage-washing between use. There are also available a variety of restraining boxes and related devices that can be used for restraint of the rabbit while an investigator is performing nonpainful manipulations, such as the induction of anesthesia.

2. Blood Collection and Venipuncture

Blood collection is usually done from the veins or arteries of the ear. Place the rabbit in a restraint box which allows for access to the ears. Disinfect the ear with 70% ethyl alcohol and apply digital pressure to the base of the ear to serve as a tourniquet. Insert a 23-gauge hypodermic needle into an auricular vein and remove the needle. The blood can then be collected directly into receptacles such as a capillary tube or microscope slide. An auricular artery can be bled to collect larger samples directly into a syringe. After collection, apply digital pressure to the collection site until bleeding has stopped and then clean the ear. Apply xylol to the ear before sample collection to engorge and dilate vessels. This chemical acts as an irritant which causes an inflammatory response and alters the cellular components of the sample. Remove the xylol first by alcohol and then by soap and water, after the sample is collected.

A method is described (Burke, 1977) whereby 60 ml of blood can be collected from an ear vein once a week. Place the rabbit in a box, stand the box on one end with the rabbit's head down, and shave the ear with a razor blade or a No. 10 surgical blade. Rub the ear vigorously with gauze saturated with xylol. Introduce a 20-gauge, 1-inch needle into the median artery. Needles longer than an inch could favor clotting. It takes about 2 minutes to collect 50–60 ml of blood. Withdraw the needle and apply firm pressure over the puncture. Let the blood stand and then centrifuge to obtain serum.

3. Cardiac Puncture

For heart blood use either a hypodermic syringe and needle, or else suck the blood through a needle leading by glass tubing directly into a container such as a 50-ml centrifuge tube. The syringe or tube should contain the correct proportions of a suitable anticoagulant.

Use a No. 18 hypodermic needle with a 1½-inch stem length (2¼ inches overall length). Swab the chest with alcohol, and palpate for the cardiac impulse. Insert the needle, watch for the needle to pulsate with each heartbeat, and then draw blood into the syringe or else suck it into the centrifuge tube (Fig. 3). About 30 ml of heart blood can be safely drawn from a 2.5-kg rabbit in an acute experiment, but if repeated samples are desired, no more than 20 ml should be drawn at intervals of 2–3 weeks. For inexperienced workers, light etherization will facilitate the procedure and should be used.

4. Intravenous Injections

Fluids can be injected i.v. into any one of several veins. The marginal or central veins of the ear are superficial and thus readily available. The anterior femoral vein in the central upper thigh is deeper and usually hidden within the fur. It is a vein of choice if an indwelling cannula is to be

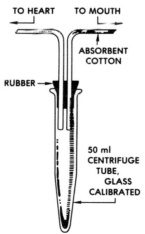

Figure 3. Blood-collection apparatus. Apparatus for collecting a large volume of blood from the heart.

used. The jugular vein is available in neck dissections where the carotid artery or cervical nerves are being exposed. The recurrent tarsal vein can be utilized; it appears as a distinct cord in the middle of the lower thigh.

5. *Heparinization*

Rabbit blood can be kept liquid by intravenous injection of at least 1000 USP units of heparin, in a single dose or in two doses of 500 units each. Single injections have only a temporary effect on the clotting time. Heparin is rapidly destroyed in blood, probably by an enzyme. The usual preparation is sodium heparin in which 2 ml contains 1000 USP units or 10 mg (1%) of heparin. Give it directly from a stock vial, or mix it with an 0.85% saline solution and slowly administer it by intravenous drip. The usual dose is 10 mg/kg of body weight. Its effects may be neutralized by intravenous injection of approximately an equal number of USP units of protamine sulfate.

For work *in vitro,* draw rabbit blood into tubes containing 10 units (0.1 mg) of heparin/ml of blood.

6. *Artificial Respiration*

In rabbit chest work, artificial respiration is ordinarily unnecessary if the sternum is opened in the exact midline since pneumothorax is not expected to occur. The thoracic cavity is separated from the atmosphere by a serous membrane that stretches between the pericardium and the lateral edges of the sternum.

In resorting to manual positive pressure methods of resuscitation, discontinue the anesthetic and rhythmically compress the thorax with the thumb and fingers of one hand. Bring the tongue forward by grasping it with gauze and swab the throat with an applicator. Occasionally, dilating the rectum with a glass rod reactivates breathing.

Our experience with manual rhythmic compression of the thorax has not been sufficiently encouraging. To obtain a somewhat more lasting effect, moderately compress the chest by wrapping rubber tubing around it, the tubing ends held together by forceps, and then gently rock the rabbit, head-up and head-down, observing whether breathing recurs.

7. *Collection of Urine*

Some investigators collect urine directly from the bladder of the intact rabbit, but the procedure seems to be more feasible in the male. Support the animal in a sitting position. Lubricate with glycerine a No. 2.9

French rubber catheter (about 1 mm O.D). Pass it into the urethra about 2 cm in a somewhat downward direction, then slightly depress the catheter and penis and push the catheter on into the bladder. Use firm abdominal pressure with the other hand to empty the bladder completely.

Before undertaking surgical procedures on the rabbit, it is advisable to actively empty its urinary bladder. This is done most simply on the supine animal by exerting manual pressure upon its lower abdomen. The pressure is exerted not only toward the animal's dorsal surface but also caudally. The animal table should be tilted so that the urine flow is aided gravitationally.

8. Depilatory Solution

The electric shaver is less effective with rabbits than with other laboratory animals because of the dense fur. An effective depilatory solution contains equal volumes of soluble starch and barium sulfide. First clip the hair with scissors; then apply the mixture with a tongue depressor to the previously wetted fur and allow a few minutes for a response. As soon as the hair is loose, wash the skin with a detergent in water; then rinse and dry it. Swab the epilated region with a freshly prepared 1:1000 aqueous solution of acriflavine, or with any other nonirritating topical antiseptic in a dosage that does not irritate the skin.

The compound called pHISOHEX (Winthrop Laboratories, New York) is an excellent antiseptic, detergent cream for preoperative hand scrubbing of the operator and for preparation of the animal's skin. The antiseptic portion of the formula is 3% hexachlorophene.

Because rabbit skin is sensitive to strong antiseptics, observe whether the application of antiseptics is consistently producing cutaneous irritation. If so, prepare the animal for surgery by shaving the skin, washing the area with soap and water, and swabbing it once with 70% alcohol.

9. Euthanasia

No animal should be subjected to procedures involving signs of distress or pain.

Euthanasia (painless death) should be performed by trained persons. The method of euthanasia should be such that it does not interfere with any postmortem examinations to be performed.

A rabbit can be killed quickly and humanely with an overdose of barbiturate solutions, given intravenously or intraperitoneally. If an inhalant anesthetic has been used to induce deep anesthesia, an overdose of the same drug can be used in any terminal experiment before the animal regains consciousness.

10. Necropsy

If the rabbit dies for any reason before the end of the experimental procedure, ascertain the cause of death.

Asphyxia due to overanesthesia is detected by the color of the tongue, by the breath odor, and by the dark color of the blood. The lungs and pleurae may show small hemorrhages indicating areas of pulmonary emphysema arising from forced inspiration. The right side of the heart is distended with blood. A froth collects in the trachea and bronchi as a result of pulmonary edema.

Shock is confusing. It may be accompanied by signs of passive congestion and a heart failure. Observe the splanchnic beds for engorgement. The spleen is relatively bloodless.

Chapter *2* Principles and Practice of Rabbit Surgery

A. PURPOSES OF SURGERY

Surgery on any living form always involves risk to life. Its performance is justified, however, for a variety of reasons: (1) It saves lives, as for example in intestinal blockage; (2) it eliminates persistent annoying disease, as in an abscess; (3) it aids in wound healing, as in lacerations; (4) it corrects anomalies of development and increases social acceptability; and (5) it leads to cosmetic improvement. These reasons hold not only in man, but extend as well to animals.

Experimental animal surgery is the basis for laying down the principles and practice of surgery in both animals and man. Historically, human surgery depended in greatest extent upon the results observed in operated animals. How would one know whether a partial gastrectomy or a splenectomy could be accomplished with considerable predictability if a historical precedent had not been established by work upon animals? Experimental animal surgery is utilized perhaps more extensively even currently in testing new materials and procedures. The complexities of such procedures as transplants or organ bypasses can be worked out first with appropriate animal models.

With respect to the student to whom this book is directed, it is of utmost importance that he or she understands surgical principles and the basic concept of humane treatment of animals before being allowed to proceed at the bench in a course involving experimental animal surgery or other experimentation with animals in mammalian physiology.

B. INTRODUCTION TO SURGICAL PRINCIPLES

The application of the following principles is required if the survival of an animal is anticipated. When the student, particularly in physiology, understands these principles and commands a working knowledge based upon them, he can proceed with operative techniques and obtain valid data.

1. *Strict asepsis.* Asepsis is critical to prevent delay in wound healing and undue animal stress. Sterile technique encompasses all aspects of the surgery room, including staff, equipment, animal preparation, and the surgical methods used.

2. *Hemostasis.* Hemorrhage must be controlled during surgery to prevent shock, maintain visibility in the operative field, and minimize postsurgical adhesions related to fibrin deposits.

3. *Exposure of surgical area.* The location and size of the incision along with positioning of the rabbit on the table must allow for clear organ presentation. The surgeon must be able to see what he is working on and particularly so that he is able to ligate vessels before emergencies (e.g., hemorrhage and shock) occur.

4. *Gentleness in tissue handling.* The physical manipulation of tissue must be delicately and properly done to prevent undue damage and delay in wound healing.

5. *Knowledge of anatomy and physiology.* To manipulate or to remove an organ, the surgeon must know such things as its form, size, shape, position, blood supply, innervation, and relationships to accomplish an orderly surgical procedure. Physiologic knowledge is required for replacement therapy and supportive aftercare.

6. *Satisfactory anesthesia.* Deep anesthesia is required for humane reasons involving the minimizing of pain. A state of immobilization and muscle relaxation is also critical for the proper execution of delicate procedures.

7. *Understanding the surgical methodology.* The appropriate sterile techniques, suturing procedures, mechanical body support systems, and instrument use are important examples of methods that must be understood.

C. STERILIZATION

Sterilization implies the complete destruction of all living matter. "Sterile" is an absolute term in that nothing can be partially sterile. Surgical sterilization is usually done either by heat or chemical means. Heat sterilization can be either moist or dry heat. Moist heat may be applied by boiling, by steam, or by steam under pressure, as in an autoclave. Dry heat may be employed by baking or flaming. Chemical sterilization is not as reliable as heat and is usually reserved for instruments that could be damaged by heat.

1. Heat Sterilization

a. Steam under Pressure. Subjecting materials to saturated steam under pressure is a dependable means for the destruction of all known forms of microbial life. The controlled application of moist heat under pressure is done in an instrument known as an autoclave. Autoclaving has the following advantages:

1. There is rapid heating and penetration of cloth materials.
2. It destroys most bacterial spores rapidly.
3. Quality and microbial lethality may be controlled for various materials by time and pressure alterations.

Autoclaves also have the following disadvantages:

1. Incomplete air elimination from the sterilizing chamber and materials depresses temperature and prevents sterilization. Air strongly opposes the diffusion and expansion of steam.
2. Incorrect operation can result in superheated steam which has diminished antimicrobial power.
3. They are not suitable for sterilization of greases, anhydrous oils, and powders.
4. They are not suitable for instruments with sharp cutting edges like scalpel blades and scissors.
5. They are not suitable for delicate instruments such as many specialized optical items.

An autoclave is a form of a pressure steam sterilizer and consists of an outer steam jacket which surrounds the load chamber, a chamber door, and a control system. The steam jacket is required to heat the chamber walls to prevent condensation in the chamber which would be caused by temperature differences. The chamber contains the materials to be sterilized, i.e., the load. The load should be arranged in the chamber to allow for the free flow of steam around all packs or materials. The safety chamber door is constructed so that it cannot be opened at autoclaving pressures. A small 20-inch diameter door has a total pressure of approximately 2.3 tons when operated at 15 p.s.i. Modern autoclaves have an electrical control system that simplifies operation.

The following sequence of events takes place during a routine autoclaving procedure:

1. Turn the steam valve on.
2. Close the condensate valve if open.
3. Push "On" button and the jacket will preheat.
4. Set the desired temperature on the dial and adjust the pressure if required (121° C or 250° F at 15 p.s.i.).
5. Load the chamber.
6. Close and lock the door.
7. Set the timer as follows:
   a. Wrapped dressing pack—30 minutes
   b. Empty glassware—15 minutes
   c. Metal instruments (no wrap)—15 minutes
   d. Instruments with double muslin wrap—30 minutes
   e. Liquids in autoclavable bottle, 250 to 500 ml—25 minutes
8. Push the desired cycle control button:
   a. "Unwrapped" button which is followed by steam injection, timed cycle at predetermined temperature and pressure, and fast exhaust of chamber
   b. "Wrapped" button which is followed by steam injection, timed cycle, fast exhaust, and vacuum drying of chamber load
   c. "Liquid" button which is followed by steam injection, timed cycle, and a slow exhaust; this allows for temperature and pressure to drop slowly so the hot liquids do not boil at a decreased pressure
   d. "Manual" button allows the user to manually select autoclave, fast exhaust, slow exhaust or vacuum dry without going through other cycles; the timer is not active during manual use and the unit must be physically turned off
9. Cycle is completed when the buzzer signals. The door can then be opened and the chamber unloaded. The material is still hot so asbestos gloves should be worn.
10. Close the door, but do not lock it.
11. Turn the unit off if it is not going to be used again on the same day.

   b. *Immersion in Boiling Water.* All instruments except sharp-pointed ones can be safely sterilized for rabbit surgery by immersion for 20 minutes in water that has already come to a boil; otherwise, they will rust. Because very sharp instruments can be dulled by boiling, it may be preferable to sterilize them chemically.

   c. *Dry Heat.* All of the material must be raised to an effective temperature for an appropriate time. Distribute the load loosely to allow free air flow. A fan inside the oven can optimize the flow.

2. Chemical

a. Phenols. These compounds are bacteriostatic or bactericidal and are active against fungi. They are not effective against spores or viruses.

The following solution is effective and will not induce rusting of instruments: phenol, 10.0–15.0 ml, formalin, 3.0 ml, boric acid, 15.0 gm, and water to 1000.0 ml.

To ensure sterility, keep instruments in this solution for 24 hours prior to use. Rinse the instruments in sterile distilled water to prevent irritation to the animal from the antiseptic.

b. Alcohol. Ethyl alcohol at 70% is a bactericide against vegetative and tubercle bacilli, but it is not effective against bacterial spores. It is useful in swabbing the skin of the operative area of the rabbit before making an incision. Isopropyl alcohol may also be used at a concentration of 90–99%.

c. Halogens. Chlorine is a useful germicide when used on clean surfaces in an acid environment. It is used for general sanitation and for surgery. Iodine in alcoholic solvent is differentially bactericidal, but not sporocidal. We use a 2% solution, or even 1% iodine in 70% ethanol to which the skin is not overly sensitive. It is best to scrub the surgical area first with soap and water since organic matter depresses iodine activity.

d. Quaternary Ammonium Compounds. These compounds are useful in sterilizing instruments and are bactericidal more against gram-positive than gram-negative organisms. In general, they are not effective against fungi, spores, or viruses.

3. Gases

a. Formaldehyde. This is an effective agent for fumigation and decontamination of surfaces. It has weak penetration, however, and is not easily removed from the surfaces. Use formaldehyde vapor at no less than 25°C (77°F) and at relative humidities not less than 70%. Irritating properties limit its surgical use.

b. Ethylene Oxide. This gas penetrates well at room temperature and low humidity. It is flammable and explosive. To eliminate its explosiveness, mix the gas with seven times its volume of carbon dioxide or use it in the absence of oxygen. The gas can be drawn into a sterilizing chamber which is first evacuated. There are commercially available ethylene oxide sterilizers that can be used for items that are not autoclavable.

4. *Filtration*

This is a practicable procedure for sterilizing heat-labile fluids. The usual filters used for liquids include asbestos pads, ultrafilters, glass filters, diatomaceous earth filters, and porcelain.

There are air filters, of fibrous or granular materials, which retain air-born particles. These are particularly useful in protecting the inlets of animal rooms.

5. *Radiation*

a. Ultraviolet. Ultraviolet radiation has low penetrating power for fluids and none for solids. Between 2800 and 2400 Å it reduces the number of organisms in air. It is seldom used in animal quarters.

b. Infrared. Infrared heating elements can sterilize syringes passing under them, if the passage lasts about 15 minutes, at 180°C or higher.

c. Ultrasonic. High frequency electricity is converted to sound waves. If such waves pass into a liquid in which microorganisms are suspended, these microorganisms can be destroyed.

D. ASSIGNMENT OF DUTIES

Each member of the team must assume a given duty for any one exercise, and he is responsible for the successful performance of his special tasks. The following assignments are suggested on a maximum basis of six students to a team. The most practicable group for rabbits should not exceed three students; in such a group there is a surgeon, anesthetist, and technician-recorder.

1. *Surgeon*

He is in general charge and is responsible for the entire experiment. He performs the principal surgery. He keeps himself informed as to the condition of the animal and decides when any manipulation is to be made.

2. Assistant Surgeon

He assists, by retracting tissues, tying knots, and by passing instruments and sponges. He watches the condition of the animal and the movements of his group members. In smaller groups he takes over the work of the surgical nurse.

3. Surgical Nurse

He prepares instruments, sponges, and drugs to be used, and has them ready when needed. He arranges the instruments and cleans them. He should not concern himself with the condition of the animal, and assists only at the request of the surgeon.

4. Recorder

He makes a complete record of everything that happens, whether it will affect the result or not. The record should show what was done, the time when it was done, and the effects of doing it.

5. Technician

He sets up all recording apparatus before the animal is worked upon. He then watches to see that everything works smoothly. In smaller groups, he takes over the work of the recorder.

6. Anesthetist

He is responsible for inducing and maintaining anesthesia and keeping the animal alive. His task is to vary anesthesia in accordance with the type of manipulation required. He informs the surgeon of any change in the condition of the animal. He watches blood pressure, respiration, and other events. He must become familiar with ether anesthesia and anesthesia with other drugs.

In order that each student may obtain manipulative experience, the positions are rotated during successive experiments.

Many exercises are not primarily surgical in method, and the members of the team may be changed in number and in assignment to fit special needs.

E. PERSONNEL PREPARATION AND SURGICAL ATTIRE

1. Surgical Arm and Hand Scrub

The skin of all persons comprising the surgical team harbors microbial organisms which could cause contamination in the wound of a rabbit. A thorough surgical scrub is required by team members before gowning. The following exemplifies an acceptable procedure:

(a) Remove all jewelry or accessories. (b) Trim and clean fingernails. (c) Put on surgical cap and mask. (d) Wet arms and hands with comfortably hot water. Wet above elbows, but do not get clothing wet. (e) Keep arms flexed with hands raised, from this point on. (f) Scrub arms and hands with liquid surgical soap. Work into a good lather and scrub until visibly clean. (g) Rinse extremities and allow water to run off your elbows. (h) Apply soap and clean under fingernails with sterile stick. Then scrub arms and hands for 5 minutes by the clock. (i) Rinse the upper extremities. (j) Apply soap and scrub in systematic fashion from nails to elbows. Scrub 5 or more minutes by the clock. (k) Rinse. (l) Repeat step j. (m) Rinse. (n) Dry hands and forearms with a sterile towel. Dry one hand and wipe arm with one end of towel and other hand and arm with other end. Take care not to recontaminate clean areas with used part of towel. (o) Keep arms flexed and hands raised and away from body. Touch sterile items listed below only.

2. Sterile Gowning

Pick up gown from open sterile pack using thumb and first finger of both hands. Grasp gown by inside shoulder folds. Back away from table and allow gown to unfold. It must not touch your clothing, floor, or room equipment. Slip hands into sleeves and extend arms. An assistant standing behind you can now assist in getting your hands through the cuffs and tying the gown. The assistant must not touch the exterior of the sleeves or the front of the gown.

3. Gloving Procedure

Take the powder envelope from the open glove pack and powder your hands. Pick up the right glove by the turned-down cuff, using the left hand. Insert your right hand into glove which is then pulled on by the left hand. The hands have touched only the inside of the glove, so the outside is still sterile (Fig. 4). Pick up the left glove by the gloved right hand. Insert the right fingers under the folded cuff of the left glove. Pull the left

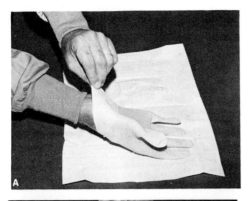

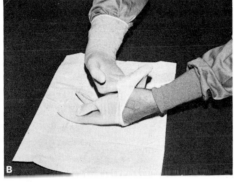

Figure 4. Gloving procedure. (A) Pick up right glove by the turned-down cuff. (B) Pick up left glove by inserting fingers in folded cuff.

glove over the gown wristlet. The left gloved hand now pulls up the right glove over the wristlet by inserting the fingers under the cuff.

For alternate methods of personnel preparation and gloving, see Lang (1976).

F. PREPARATION OF THE SURGICAL FIELD IN THE RABBIT

Determine the exact location of the incision before "prepping" the animal for surgery. It is advantageous to anesthetize the rabbit in a surgical preparation room. Shave the area of the incision with electric clippers. The clipper blade must be one specified for Angora fur since the more common No. 40 surgical blade with closer teeth becomes matted on rabbit fur. The No. 40 blade can be used for final clipping if residual fur

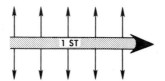

Figure 5.   Skin preparation. Swab first along incision line and then radiate outward to cover the shaved field. Do not recontaminate incision line.

remains. After electric clipping, lather the area with surgical soap and shave that area with a sharp razor. With practice, a straight razor can be used, but a safety razor with a new blade works sufficiently well for general classroom use. The area shaved should be large enough to prevent later contamination by uncut fur. Use depilatory compounds as previously outlined if other shaving equipment is not available. After the area is fur-free, scrub it with a surgical soap using gauze squares as the scrub cloth. It must be emphasized that rabbit skin does not tolerate brush scrubbing. Rinse the area with large volumes of water. Transport the rabbit to the surgery room and position it on the table in the desired plane. Scrub the surgical area with soap and rinse it. Repeat as often as needed until the area looks clean.

Wipe the incision line with 70% ethyl alcohol and then continue this maneuver progressively peripheral to the incision line without touching the area to be incised (Fig. 5). Allow the alcohol to air dry for 5 minutes, then swab the area again in the same fashion, substituting a 2% iodine solution. The rabbit is then ready for draping.

G. SURGICAL DRAPING

The fur and skin of the rabbit surrounding the area sterilized are a prime potential source of contaminants. This can be minimized by the use of sterile drapes to cover the skin surrounding the prepared incision line. Drapes of many sizes and shapes can be used. There are commercial, disposable drape packs that are sterilized and ready for use. Shop-type hand towels also work well if properly prepared. Four towels autoclaved in a pack suffice for most procedures. They should be accordian-folded to facilitate later handling. The "sterile" surgeon places one towel crosswise and caudal to the incision site, one cranial to the site, and one towel on each side of the site. Use towel clamps to hold the drapes in place. Clamp each towel on the fold under the main 'body drape, so the clamps are not exposed. This helps to maintain a clear surgical field (Fig. 6).

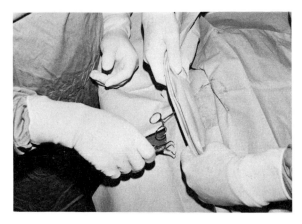

Figure 6. Draping. Sterile drapes should cover the rabbit and towel clamps should not be exposed to the operative field.

H. SURGICAL INSTRUMENTS

1. Surgical Needles

Surgical needles are either *eyed needles* into which the suture is threaded or *eyeless* which are firmly fastened to the suture. Both types are available in many forms and sizes (Fig. 7).

Round-bodied, noncutting needles are useful in suturing thin membranes which may easily tear. The *triangular-shaped* cutting needles are more useful for thicker tissues, e.g., skin or fascia. Straight needles are available in a variety of lengths and also with cutting or noncutting points.

The *half-curved* needles have half the needle curved and the other half straight, and they have either round or triangular shafts.

The *half-circle* needles are curved throughout their length, forming a semicircle. They also have either round or triangular bodies. The *3/8 circle* needle is a variation of the half-circle type.

To thread a needle, pull the suture through the eye at least 4 inches.

Figure 7. Surgical needles. (A) Straight, (B) half-curved, (C) half-circle, (D) 3/8 circle, (E) noncutting needle point, and (F) cutting needle.

Thread curved needles from within the curvature so that the short end of the suture falls from the outside curvature. To partially secure the suture material in the needle, you can thread the needle twice, forming a band around the shaft.

Sterilize needles by chemical means, since heating will dull the points and limit their useful life-span.

2. Needle Holders

Needle holders have a wide variety of designs. The tips may be blunt or tapered. They may have to be closed by manual pressure or with ratchets. Use the holder to grip the needle while suturing, to provide extra force for needle penetration of tissues, and to allow visibility of the area being sutured (Fig. 8).

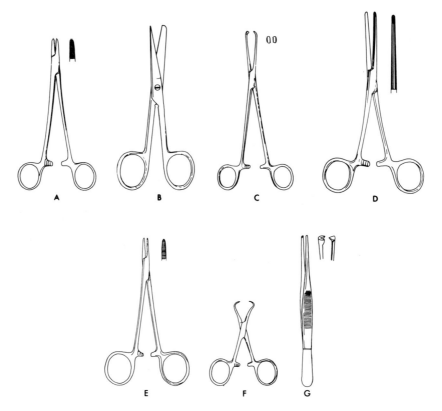

Figure 8. Surgical instruments. (A) Needle holder, (B) blunt–sharp scissors, (C) Allis tissue forceps, (D) Carmalt forceps, (E) Halsted hemostatic forceps, (F) Backhaus' towel clips, and (G) thumb tissue forceps.

3. Scissors

Scissors have a wide variety of shapes and sizes. The ends of scissors may be blunt or sharp or combinations of the two. They are therefore described as blunt–blunt, blunt–sharp, and sharp–sharp. There are also curved and straight scissors. There are many varieties of scissors used for special purposes such as stitch scissors, bandage scissors, wire scissors, iris scissors, serrated scissors, and others.

4. Forceps

Forceps are pincerlike instruments designed for grasping, crushing, or extracting. There is a wide variety of types. Tissue forceps have fine, sharp teeth, and are useful for holding skin and subcutaneous tissues with a minimum of trauma. The Allis forceps is an example. There are tissue forceps whose ends have serrated jaws for crushing, which produces tissue necrosis. Kelly, Cushing, and Halstead forceps are examples.

5. Retractors

Retractors are necessary to separate the margins of a wound to allow good visualization (adequate exposure) of the field of operation.

Some of these instruments are manually retractable and some are self-retractable. The latter retain their position after placement.

6. Scalpels

The scalpel is the major instrument used. The common type is the steel handle which accommodates a disposable blade. Number 3 handle will hold Nos. 10, 11, 12, and 15 blades. Number 4 handle will hold Nos. 20, 21, 22, 23, 24, and 25 blades. Blade numbers describe the blade shape and size.

7. Towel Clips

There are several varieties of towel clips (e.g., Gray's, Doyen's, Backhaus', Mayo's, Moynihan's) and they resemble forceps. They secure sterile towels in place about the surgical area.

8. Curettes, Scoops, and Spoons

Curettes, scoops, and spoons vary from large to small, hollow to solid, and rounded to soft, depending upon the type of surgical procedure. In bone surgery the scoops and spoons have sharp, cutting edges and are used for scraping bones.

9. *Trocars and Cannulas*

There are many types and uses of trocars and cannulas, adapted, for example, to the gallbladder, ovary, and sinuses. Some are for draining subcutaneous tissues of fluid. The tracheal cannula is particularly useful in the rabbit connected into tracheostomy openings because of the considerable difficulty in attempting to pass the common cuffed endotracheal cannula.

Clean and dry cannulas after each use to ensure patency of the lumen, prior to sterilization and storage.

10. *Clamps*

Clamps are instruments to produce compression. They include as examples Parker's duodenal clamps, Spencer-Wells' kidney pedicle clamps, Payr's intestinal clamps, and Moynihan's gallbladder clamps.

11. *Cleaning the Instruments*

Wash instruments thoroughly in cold water. Soap or detergent can be added. For forceps with serrated jaws, use a brush to remove debris and blood. Sterilize and dry the instruments.

Store instruments in dry places and in such a way as to prevent them from considerable mutual contact. Lubricate the joints of instruments having movable parts.

Clean syringes even if they are new. Wash and brush their barrels, rinse them in water and dry them. Lightly smear the piston with paraffin and push the piston along the barrel several times. Then rinse the syringes with cold water. Wash used syringes in cold water containing a detergent and antiseptic and do this quickly after use to avoid sticking of the piston.

I. SUTURES, LIGATURES, AND KNOTS

A *suture* is a fine, cordlike structure used to close wounds. The term is used to denote either the material that is used, as gut or silk, or the method of using the material such as a simple interrupted stitch. A *ligature* is a cord or strand employed to tie off blood vessels or other structures. Ligation is the act of tying or binding.

The margins of a surgical wound are entirely dependent upon sutures to keep them approximated, for the first three to four postsurgical days. Fibroplasia begins about the fourth day and the process produces a maximum binding strength about the twelfth to fourteenth postsurgical day.

It is apparent that sutures serve a critical role in the healing of surgical wounds. The effectiveness of the suture depends on the suture material, suture pattern, handling of suture material before use, and suture technique.

The most important consideration in wound suturing is the "holding power" of the tissue and not the strength of the suture material (Mayer *et al.*, 1957). The ability of a tissue to hold sutures without danger of tissue tearing depends on the density of the tissue and the direction of pull of the sutures. The strength of a suture line increases in proportion to the number of sutures, but only to a certain point. Assuming a given intrinsic tissue holding power, a strong suture line strength is reached when the sutures are approximately 0.5 cm apart. Suture line strength can still be increased, however, by increasing the size of the "bite" (distance from incision to needle penetration).

1. Absorbable Sutures

Absorbable sutures are enzymatically digested (absorbed) after a number of days of healing by the tissues in which they are embedded. *Surgical gut* (catgut), a collagen which is derived from the lamb's small intestine, is most frequently used.

The rate of digestion of catgut by the enzymes of the host can be retarded by treating catgut with chromic acid. This *chromicized surgical gut*, which can be mild, medium, or extra chromic (Type B, C, or D), retains its integrity much longer than *plain gut* (Type A). Surgical gut absorption time is controlled by the amount of chromic acid and not by the diameter of the material. Type C (medium) chromic gut should remain intact 10–20 days when placed in striated muscle.

Nonboilable catgut is generally received in cans or glass jars in which the suture tubes are surrounded by 70% ethanol plus formaldehyde solution and is ready for use. There is a *boilable* gut, currently in much less use, which has been dried and sealed in glass tubes with an anhydrous solvent such as xylol. The absence of water allows the gut to be heated in the tube without "cooking" it. This gut can have its tube exterior sterilized by autoclaving. It is immersed in sterile water for a few minutes to prepare it for surgical use. It is weaker than the nonboilable type.

Since small sizes of gut produce less reaction and irritation than large sizes do, use the size that is consistent with the strength of the tissue in which it is to be placed.

Catgut is numbered in gauges according to the diameter of the strands and to their tensile strength.

2. Nonabsorbable Sutures

Nonabsorbable sutures remain in tissues for variably long periods of time. This type includes silk, cotton, nylon, linen, and metallic wires. The metals are silver, stainless steel, and tantalum. Silk, linen, and cotton are slowly destroyed in the tissues.

Surgical silk sutures are generally dyed black to be more visible in tissues. They are usually noncapillary, which means that they prevent either moisture or bacterial penetration into the woven threads. The silk is commonly braided to add tensile strength and it is available on spools. It should be cut in suitable lengths from the spool and wrapped around tubes or tongue depressors. Silk is autoclavable.

Cotton sutures are twisted fibers with a smooth surface and are weak in comparison with silk. The sutures come on spools or in precut lengths. They should not be sterilized on the original spool, because of shrinkage. They have some capillary action and are difficult to handle.

There is an *artificial silkworm gut* (Dermal) which is a twisted silk, coated with a tanned gelatin or other protein which can be autoclaved.

Nylon suture is a high-tensile, flexible, smooth synthetic, supplied braided or in strands. Nylon is sterilized by autoclaving. It is destroyed by phenol preparations including Lysol.

Metal sutures include several varieties of metals, the preferred ones being stainless steel and tantalum. Metals are noncapillary and nonirritating to tissues.

Tantalum is inert, nonirritating, pliable, and has a high tensile strength. It is supplied as wire, wire gauze, ribbons, plates, and screws. The metal is sterilized by autoclaving.

Stainless steel is supplied as wire, steel gauze, plates, and screws. The metal is sterilized by autoclaving.

Note: The chief disadvantage of the organic nonabsorbable sutures is

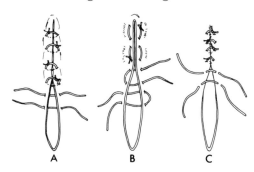

        A   B   C

Figure 9. Interrupted suture patterns. (A) Simple, (B) horizontal mattress, and (C) Lembert.

their tendency to cause wound sinuses. This is seen in the subcutaneous tissue. In the deeper layers, silk and linen give rise to less trouble. This type of suture loses tensile strength rapidly after about two months. It gets very fragile in about 6 months.

Use nonabsorable sutures in such strong fascial layers as the rectus muscle sheath and the external oblique aponeurosis. Fascia heals slowly whereas catgut is absorbed too soon.

It is good practice to use interrupted sutures where stability and strength are needed in a suture line. Then if one suture breaks or a knot unties, the consequences may be small (Figs. 9 and 10).

3. Surgical Knots

There are only a few types of knots used in basic surgery. Dexterity and speed should be developed in tying a square knot and a surgeon's knot. Both hand and instrument ties are required and should be practiced (Figs. 11 and 12).

Good knot-tying technique requires that

1. All finished knots must be firm and unable to slip.
2. The knot must be small to minimize tissue reaction.
3. A seesaw or friction motion which weakens suture material must be avoided.
4. Excessive tension should not be applied in suturing or knot tying. This enables the surgeon to use finer gauge material with less inflammation.
5. Sutures should not cause tissue strangulation except for vessel ligation.
6. Many ligatures are often required to maintain perfect hemostasis and extra ties on a square knot only add more foreign material.

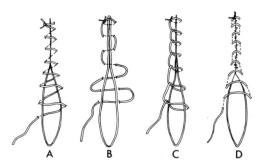

A   B   C   D

Figure 10.   Continuous suture patterns. (A) Simple, (B) horizontal mattress, (C) blanket or lock stitch, and (D) Cushing.

Detailed descriptions of suturing and knot tying techniques are given in "Manual of Operative Procedure and Surgical Knots," (1968).

Simple knot, square knot, and surgeon's knot are illustrated in Fig. 13.

J. WOUND HEALING

Damage to tissues, including that caused by surgery, is followed by a generally predictable series of responses, the first set called *inflammation*

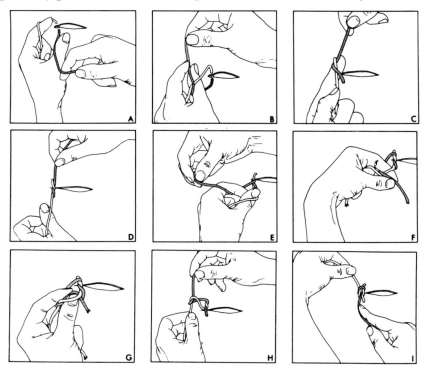

Figure 11.　Hand tie. Tying a square knot by hand.

and the second *repair*. There is no sharp division temporally between these sets of responses. Our emphasis is on repair.

1. Cellular Aspects of Repair

If regeneration of tissue were perfect, all functional cells characteristic of the tissue would be replaced. Regeneration becomes limited in the evolutionary process, however. This is seen in wound healing where there is the utilization of nonspecific connective tissue elements, with the for-

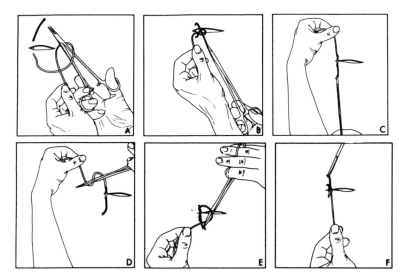

Figure 12. Instrument tie. Tying a square knot with instrument.

mation of fibrous scar tissue. This decreases the reserve of an organ or tissue.

The replacement of cells by like reserves occurs only if such cells retain a capacity for mitotic divisions. *Permanent* cells, such as ganglion cells, and smooth and striated muscle cells, do not undergo mitotic division. In myocardial infarction, there is scarring and loss of cardiac reserve. A neuron cannot divide, although its cell body can redevelop any of its extended processes.

There are, fortunately, *labile* cells which multiply throughout life. These include epithelial, hematopoietic, and lymphoid cells. Such cells have an enormous capacity to replace themselves.

A third type includes *stable* cells. These are usually quiescent, but they are potentially able to regenerate themselves. This category includes the

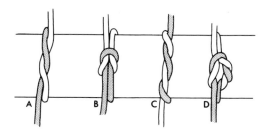

Figure 13. Knots. (A) Simple knot, (B) square knot, (C) surgeon's knot, and (D) surgeon's knot completed.

parenchymal cells of all the visceral organs. The great capacity of liver cells to restore themselves is an outstanding example, although this is accomplished with the supplementary help of the fibrous connective tissue cells. All mesenchymal cells as well as their derivatives fall into the category of stable cells; the fibroblasts are an important example. In healing, many of the mesenchymal cells can differentiate into specific elements needed for a given tissue. Thus, chondroblasts and osteoblasts form from such precursors.

The potential for mitosis is clearly a necessary factor in wound healing. It is also necessary that the basic stromal architecture of a tissue not be severely disrupted. Restoration of mass without framework is followed by imperfect function.

In damage to most tissues, fibroblasts, other cells, and young blood capillaries migrate into the wound. The resulting deep-red tissue with a somewhat granular appearance is called *granulation tissue*. The cells of this tissue proliferate, the fibroblasts converting to collagen fibrils which bring about permanent union. The new formation of blood vessels occurs from preexisting vessels.

The visible mass in the breach of the wound is a *scar*. The scar represents the replacement of the original tissue by connective tissue. It constitutes an efficient reparative process despite the variable loss of specialized parenchymal cell function.

As the healing proceeds, the cells brought in gradually become reduced in size. Some disappear, while others are converted. Many of the newly formed capillaries close and ultimately disappear. It is this predictable series of events that is described as either *primary* or *secondary union*. The purpose of either type of union is to restore form, strength, and function. Restoration to full normalcy is a reasonable expectation and especially so in generalized tissues.

a. Primary Union. This type of healing is typified in surgical incisions where the opposing edges are drawn together by sutures. This minimizes the chances of infection and shortens the duration of the inflammatory process.

A blood clot fills the suture line, sealing the wound. The fibroblasts and capillaries crisscross the deeper levels of the gap. Epithelial cells bridge the surface, having their origin in basal cell divisions and basal cell migrations. Specialized cells, comprising hair follicles, sweat glands, and sebaceous glands, may not be replaced. The proliferating blood vessels are gradually compressed by fibroblasts and the redness of the scar fades. The fibroblasts convert to collagen and many fibroblasts disappear. The tensile strength of the wound builds up in a few weeks, but is completed only after 1 to 2 months. It is the collagen that provides most of the tensile strength. Whether the repair is by primary or secondary union, the predominant features involve fibroplasia and vascularization.

b. Secondary Union. This activity involves healing from the bottom of the wound up to the surface, a process made necessary where there is a large gap between the edges of the wound. There is the necessity to remove all necrotic debris resulting from inflammation or traumatic destruction. The gap is then filled by ingrowth of vascularized connective tissue which becomes increasingly collagenous. The floor of the wound contains actively forming capillaries which loop upward toward the surface. The fibroblasts are at first chiefly parallel to the capillaries. Granulocytes emigrate from the upper aspects of the new capillaries and travel to the surface where they play an antibacterial role.

In the more advanced stage, the fibroblasts reorient to lie parallel to the surface. The fibroblasts produce collagen in the same plane and these fibers contract, thus reducing the surface area of the wound. The fibrous matrix forms from below upward.

The granulation tissue invades the area often while the inflammatory process in the center of the wound is still active. The epithelial cells at the wound margins proliferate and grow over the vascular tissue. If the covering is complete, the granulocytes disappear, leaving mononuclear leukocytes. The epithelium increases in depth and differentiation, devascularization continues, collagen orients along the stress lines, and the tissue becomes dense and fibrous (the white scar).

It is emphasized that the wound gap is filled not only by vascularized connective tissue, but also by the process of *contraction*.

Scar tissue is a prominent feature in secondary union and it normally fades when fibroblast pressures compress the capillaries. Also, the development of collagen helps to eliminate the vessels.

2. *Aberrations in Wound Healing*

There are aberrations that may occur in healing whether by first or second union. The term *contraction* is not an aberration since it is a normal aspect, particularly of secondary union. *Contracture* is abnormal. It involves excessive scar formation and subsequent distortions in wound closure. Scar tissue has very little elasticity to remain expanded and it usually assumes an unacceptable shape. Such tissue contracts overly.

If collagen is laid down excessively, a protruding scar, called a *keloid*, can result. If it is granulation tissue that is produced excessively, this tissue rises above the skin, blocking reepithelialization. This, in human pathology, is *proud flesh*.

3. Internal Wound Healing

All tissues of the body heal in the same ways as described for surface wounds. The connective tissue repair predominates where perfect parenchymal regeneration does not suffice for repair. Vascularized connective tissue replacement followed by laying down of collagen is the process utilized.

4. Gross Signs of Healing

Healthy granulation tissue is a thin, firm, bright-red membrane, with a granular surface that does not bleed easily and which has no offensive odor. There is very little fluid exudation from its surface. The contiguous areas show no signs of irritation. The presence of multiple signs, including pain, a foul smell, exudation, bleeding, and unusual color and swelling is an indication of unhealthy granulation tissue.

5. Factors Affecting Healing

Many factors affect the healing of wounds. Some factors are under the control of the operator and others not.

The intensity and duration of the injurious influence are important. Age influences healing. The immunologic status is especially important in the control of microbiologic infections. An adequate blood supply permits a more effective inflammatory reaction. The specific genetically determined mitotic regenerative capacity differentially affects the healing of different tissues.

Some important factors that impair healing include lymphatic obstruction, poor blood supply, and the presence of foreign bodies. Steroids, particularly cortisol, delay healing.

Nutrition is a cardinal consideration in wound repair, although foods appear to be preferentially directed toward wounds in the presence of dietary deficiency. Probably the most important factor is the need for proteins. In severe protein deficiency there is a decrease in fibroplasia and in the deposition of collagen, leading to a lack of tensile strength. If the deficiency is particularly in the amino acids containing sulfhydryl groups, enzyme reactions are depressed.

Vitamins affect regeneration. The B vitamins, which form coenzymes, promote cellular metabolism. Vitamin C is especially important in the process leading to the formation of collagen.

6. Regeneration of Specific Tissues or Organs

Epithelium and mucous membranes have marked power of regeneration. Their highly specialized derivatives, e.g., hair follicles, are not fully regenerated. Serous membranes, e.g., peritoneum, regenerate easily. Specialized epithelia have considerable power of hypertrophy and hyperplasia.

Liver and *kidney* wounds are repaired by proliferation of their own specialized cells, along with the rapid proliferation of fibrous tissue. Repeated partial hepatectomy is followed quickly by enlargement of the remaining parts of the liver. In a few weeks there is remarkable restoration to full size and architecture. In destruction of the convoluted tubules of the kidney, the surviving cells can produce the repair without connective tissue growth.

Muscle cells of all types are claimed not to be able to regenerate, but there are some challenges to this view. Connective tissue cells and new blood vessels fill the gap and unite the ends of severed muscles. In cardiac and smooth muscle, repair takes place by the use of white fibrous tissue. Smooth muscle cells may proliferate to some extent by mitosis. The hypertrophy of the uninjured muscle fibers of all types accounts for the virtual replacement of an original muscle mass, although in smooth muscle there may be the limited additional process of proliferation of muscle cells.

Connective tissue formation after damage takes place rapidly and becomes excessive if damage to or loss of new cells is repeated. Both elastic and fibrous tissue regenerate easily. Elastic tissue may be defective in wound healing; thus its special arrangements in the skin may not be restored. In the intima of arteries, new elastic laminae with regular arrangements occur.

Cartilage usually heals slowly because of avascularity. The regenerative capacity varies with the location. Articular cartilage does not regenerate. Costal cartilage regenerates if the perichondrium is intact. In general, cartilage cells have little power of proliferation. Either new cartilage cells are produced from the perichondrium or young connective tissue cells and capillaries grow in.

Bone has a remarkable capacity for regeneration. There is active proliferation of osteoblasts to occupy the gap. The osteoblasts then form a matrix, just as collagenous fibers are deposited by connective tissue cells. In continuing damage there is excessive formation of dense sclerotic bone which is the analogue of scar tissue.

Blood cells are regenerated relatively quickly and completely if precursors are made available.

Capillaries are regenerated rapidly and become excessive when there is repeated damage to or loss of new cells. Endothelial cells proliferate rapidly, as seen when needed to supply new capillaries or to repair a surface that has been desquamated.

Nerve cells when injured do not regenerate. Axons of a severed nerve regenerate if the neurilemma sheath is present and if the cell body of the neuron is intact. The axon is dependent upon the integrity of the cell body. The neurilemma cells act to guide the new nerve fibers originating from the central end.

Neuroglia cells regenerate easily and provide for repair within the central nervous system if the lesion affects neural tissue only.

K. POSTSURGICAL CARE AND EMERGENCIES

1. Replacement of Nutrients

Following surgery there is lysis of cellular protoplasm. The products are released into the extracellular fluids, some are changed to glucose and oxidized, and considerable nitrogen is excreted as urea in the urine. Skeletal muscle cells are especially involved because of temporary immobilization and decreased food intake. The release of cell products accounts for a negative nitrogen balance (chiefly as urea of the urine), the appearance of new glucose, a decreased power to synthesize new muscle protein, the occurrence in the urine of increased muscle substances such as creatine, creatinine, and uric acid, and the loss of cell mineral ions (especially potassium, phosphate, and sulfate).

The catabolic events in muscle are not reflected importantly in the total cell mass of brain, heart, lungs, kidneys, intestine, and liver, and even muscle recovers fully. The loss of nitrogen and body fat does not need to affect the healing of wounds or the production of such compounds as albumin or hemoglobin. Wounds can heal well in the catabolic phase unless starvation follows wound injury.

The body upon injury tends to emphasize conservation of volume of the extracellular fluids even more than it does maintenance of chemical concentrations. Less sodium is lost in urine, saliva, and sweat, and this factor causes retention of body water. A tendency toward oliguria is another conserving mechanism. These facts indicate that there is reason for moderation in administering sodium and water after surgery. The amount given should be that which maintains normal blood volume and hematocrit and which allows normal renal flow. In the excessive use of sodium transfusions and retention, potassium and hydrogen ions are excreted or passed into cells. An extracellular alkalosis may follow.

If there is severe injury, acute starvation may occur. The animal can shift to endogenous burning of lipids, using these to satisfy its energy requirements. This is reflected in a fall in the R. Q. (0.7) and a rise in blood glucose. For the first few hours after severe surgery, glycogen supplies carbohydrate energy.

The postoperative animal may fail to excrete sodium bicarbonate. The blood can then be alkalotic and the urine acidotic. This appears to be a stress effect in which adrenal cortex aldosterone retains sodium while excreting potassium and hydrogen ions.

The anabolic phase in postsurgical recovery takes two or three weeks because of compensating for a large total nitrogen loss. Primary wound healing goes on before there is restoration of positive nitrogen balance. The balance can be slowed down if exercise is excessive.

When muscle mass is restored, as indicated by return of nitrogen metabolism to zero balance, weight gain can occur, under conditions of moderate exercise, by a gain in body fat. This may require dietary control.

It is unnecessary to supply a highly concentrated input of nutrients in the convalescent animal. The tissues meet their needs for a few days by endogenous metabolism. In the immediate postsurgical period the need for calories is low and food should not be forced. The diet needs management in the convalescent period of slow return to nitrogen balance. The rabbit can resume its usual diet in late convalescence to maintain the positive nitrogen balance that has been reached.

Where postoperative infusions of nutrients appear advisable, the following principles apply. Postoperative infusion of easily utilizable glucose provides 4 calories per gram. A 125-ml solution of 5% (isotonic) glucose provides only about 25 calories, but builds up extracellular volume. Glucose can be replaced by 10% fructose.

2. Other Postsurgical Care

Following surgery, in survival exercises, the rabbit needs special care, especially while recovering from the anesthetic. Place the animal in a special recovery area, in a cage by itself, in a position of lateral recumbency with head extended. Because of a lowered metabolism and body temperature, it may be advisable to lay it on a warm pad or to use a heat lamp. If a large dose of barbiturates prolongs the period of recovery from anesthesia, turn the rabbit every hour. Although abdominal bandaging is advisable to prevent the rabbit from tearing out sutures, the bandage must not be so tight that it occludes venous return.

3. Management of Shock

Circulatory shock means generalized inadequacy of blood flow resulting in damage to tissues. The cause is usually insufficient cardiac output. There are several types of shock, i.e., hemorrhagic, neurogenic, anaphylactic, septic, and traumatic. Peripheral circulatory impairment or failure is a common characteristic of all types of shock.

The term "surgical shock" may be applied to shock that occurs following surgery. Surgical shock may be caused by the loss of extracellular fluid, severe tissue damage, severe pain (unwarranted in experimental work), or hemorrhage, and the shock state is often compounded by general anesthesia.

The signs of shock in the rabbit are variable and are importantly determined by the underlying causes. The rabbit may display a rapid thready pulse, rapid breathing, thirst, decrease in body temperature, lowered blood pressure, and oliguria. As hypoxia increases, a blue discoloration of mucous membranes (cyanosis) appears. Hemoconcentration can be demonstrated by a hematocrit determination if the shock state was not caused by hemorrhage.

It is important to recognize the existence and stage of shock and to start treatment prior to any other therapy except hemorrhage control. As with any circulatory failure, adequate tissue oxygenation is critical. Administer oxygen in high concentration by inhalation. Allow the rabbit to breathe up to 100% oxygen from a face mask or, less efficiently, through an intranasal tube. Remember that in a circulatory deficiency the value of this therapy alone is decreased because the oxygen is not easily delivered by the impaired blood flow.

An injection of a sympathomimetic drug, e.g., epinephrine or norepinephrine can be attempted. This technique is controversial even though such drugs increase the vasomotor tone throughout the body and counteract the histaminic effects in anaphylactic shock.

Replacement therapy is rational. In hemorrhage the best fluid replacement would be the transfusion of whole blood, but the usual lack of availability negates this approach or, for that matter, even the use of plasma. However, plasma expanders, e.g., dextran, are commercially available and they perform the same hemodynamic functions as plasma.

For progressive signs of dehydration, administer an appropriate electrolyte solution by intravenous drip. Supply the necessary components by chemical analysis of a sample of blood. Surgical suites should include access to a clinical laboratory.

4. Postsurgical Infections

Postsurgical infections should receive immediate attention. Evaluate the overall procedure and attempt to identify possible reasons for infection. Consider all aspects of sterilization, preparation, and the surgical procedure along with possible errors related to aftercare. Use antibiotics when needed as indicated by sensitivity testing, but do not use antibiotics to replace good surgical technique.

5. Herniation

A postsurgical hernia occurs when the peritoneum, muscle, and fascia separate along a suture line, allowing the opening to be penetrated by an internal organ. A hernia indicates improper suturing, anatomic weakness, or physiologic alterations that prevent proper wound healing. Repair a hernia by reincising the skin and reconstructing the internal suture line. The corrective action does require that freshly cut surfaces are available for apposition to promote wound healing by first intention.

6. Evisceration

Evisceration occurs when a suture line separation involves all layers of the abdominal wall including the skin, followed by prolapse of the abdominal viscera. Closure of wounds that have been disrupted in this fashion is difficult because the tissue becomes contaminated, edematous, and so friable that new sutures will not hold. Prevent evisceration instead of attempting to treat it; if it should occur, euthanatize the rabbit.

Chapter 3 Principles and Applications of Rabbit Anesthesia

RABBIT ANESTHESIA

The purpose of anesthesia is for immobilization and to render the rabbit insensitive to pain. Adequate anesthesia is a prerequisite for surgery. The following discussion refers to *general* anesthesia which is to be differentiated from other types such as *local* or *regional* anesthesia. Pulse, respiration, body temperature, and other signs must be continually monitored to determine the depth of anesthesia that has been induced.

General anesthesia is broken down into four temporal stages for descriptive purposes. There is overlap between stages and all rabbits will not react identically. All general anesthetic agents must be administered to *effect* while the operator evaluates total body functions. The following is a general description of the stages:

Stage I. Analgesia. This stage extends from the beginning of anesthetic administration to the loss of full consciousness. It is evidenced by a progressive loss of signs of pain. The rabbit will often show voluntary excitement during this stage.

Stage II. Excitement. This stage extends from loss of consciousness to the beginning of regular breathing. The stage is characterized by breath-holding, accelerated pulse and blood pressure, and involuntary struggling. The animal is disoriented. Sensations appear to be highly misrepresented and excitement may occur with or without external stimulation.

Stage III. Surgical anesthesia. The entry into this stage is characterized by the onset of rhythmic breathing which is under automatic, subcerebral control. Muscle relaxation increases as the anesthetic stage deepens. State III is divided into four planes:

Plane 1. Both costal and abdominal respiratory movements are active and the rate may increase. The eyelid reflex is decreased or abolished. The eyeball may oscillate and then become eccentrically stationary. The pedal reflex decreases.

Plane 2. The eyeball becomes concentrically fixed. Breathing is regular and deep, but slower than in Plane 1. The pupils may dilate. There is a slight pedal reflex. Most surgery can be carried out in Plane 1 or 2.

Plane 3. Costal breathing begins to decrease as a result of decreasing nerve impulses to the chest muscles. Diaphragmatic (abdominal muscle) activity becomes more prominent to compensate for the costal muscle depression. There is a rapid inspiration with prolonged expiration. Pupillary dilation increases. The pedal reflex is lost. This is *deep surgical* anesthesia.

Plane 4. Costal muscle activity is completely depressed. The thorax may be immobile or the intercostal spaces may retract at inspiration. Breathing is abdominal (diaphragmatic). The breathing movements are arrythmic and are characterized by short, gasping inspirations followed by prolonged expirations.

Stage IV. Respiratory arrest (medullary). The diaphragm is paralyzed. This is followed by asphyxia and death.

In the ordinary course of events, recovery from anesthesia is in the reverse order of induction of anesthesia. The surgical team should always be prepared for anesthetic emergencies. If Stage IV is entered, take the following actions:

1. Discontinue the administration of all anesthetic agents.
2. Pull out the tongue and maintain open airways. Use a mechanical respirator or artificial respiration to rhythmically drive the thorax.
3. Inject chemical agents that are respiratory stimulants.
4. Use pure oxygen via a tank and face mask.
5. When the emergency has passed, administer, if necessary, agents to correct the fluid balance, to aid in the detoxification activities of the liver, and to promote diuresis.

Rabbits should be put into Stage III of anesthesia before any surgical procedure is undertaken upon them. The student must become thoroughly familiar with the stages of anesthesia for any anesthetic he uses.

For the rabbit, satisfactory inhalation and injection anesthetic agents are available. The dosages vary with age and breed and any given drug is best standardized on one breed. We prefer the New Zealand white rabbit. A number of procedures are described herein, but the list is not exhaustive. The reader is referred to a review of agents and procedures in Lumb and Jones (1973).

1. Preparation of Rabbits

It is advisable to keep a rabbit off feed for at least 24 hours prior to surgery and, for some procedures, to withhold water for 12 hours. Do not withhold water for young or aged rabbits. An empty alimentary canal is desirable for manipulations and it minimizes abdominal and diaphragmatic pressures which could restrict breathing. Any rabbit with signs of illness should not be used for surgery or for valid and reliable data collection. The rabbit can be allowed to move freely prior to induction of anesthesia to permit urination and defecation.

2. Inhalation Anesthesia

In this route volatile liquids or gases can be used. Effective anesthetics for the rabbit are ether, halothane, methoxyflurane, or certain combinations used with injection anesthetics. The volatile agents are rapidly excreted, primarily by lung exhalation, thus allowing good control of depth by the anesthetist.

a. Ether. This volatile liquid (ethyl ether; diethyl ether) has been recommended in some exercises herein since it is a basic agent which illustrates clearly the four major stages of anesthesia (I, analgesia; II, excitement; III, surgical anesthesia; and IV, respiratory paralysis).

Ether has disadvantages. *It is explosive.* It can lead to the rapid development of pulmonary edema. Also, a rabbit exposed to an irritant vapor may hold its breath until it dies. In many cases the rapid breathing that follows breath holding will cause rapid progression to Stage IV and death if ether delivery is not stopped. This is unique to the rabbit.

Generally, in using anesthetics, if the rabbit blinks spontaneously, it may be underanesthetized, and this is also indicated by swallowing movements, rapid and forceful breathing, and a rigid abdomen. Overanesthesia is evidenced by shallow, feeble breathing, by the changing color of the tongue, and by a bluish tinge to the blood issuing from a surgical incision.

Anesthesia should be deepened when opening the peritoneum, and lightened after it is opened.

Because of the depression of the body temperature and metabolism with anesthetics such as ether, it is sometimes advisable to keep the animal warm, as by a rubber hot-water container placed under the animal. Although heating devices are useful when the students are inexperienced, these devices can later be dispensed with.

A simple method to administer an inhalation anesthetic such as ether is by "open drop." Drop the anesthetic continually onto gauze in a mask which is held over the nose and mouth. The inhaled air vaporizes the drug. Another adequate device is a metal cone, open at both ends, with absorbent cotton or gauze stuffed loosely into the narrow apical end; these cones are commercially available in several sizes. Nose cones should be large enough to cover nose and mouth. In the open-drop procedure, use of an ophthalmic ointment in the eyes to avoid drying and irritation is recommended, although not essential.

b. Halothane and Methoxyflurane. Halothane is nonexplosive and nonflammable. Methoxyflurane will not explode at room temperature, but it can do so at temperatures higher than those used clinically. It can be used with electric cautery. Induction by methoxyflurane alone is slow and restraint becomes a problem. Halothane (fluothane) because of high vapor pressure is conveniently used in a "closed rebreathing system." Carbon dioxide is removed by an absorber as the exhaled halothane anesthetic flows through the instrument. Halothane is vaporized, mixed with oxygen, and delivered via tubing to face mask. The inspired concentration of the drug can be reduced from about 5% during induction to about 1% for maintenance.

A homemade closed circuit apparatus to deliver halothane is described by Skartvedt and Lyon (1972). Compressed air is forced through tubing to vaporize the anesthetic. A flowmeter monitors the incident airflow. The final concentration of the air–anesthetic mixture is adjusted by a bypass needle valve. The rabbit is initially anesthetized in a clear plastic box into which the flowing anesthetic is introduced. The rabbit is then removed and connected to a face mask at the outlet of the box. Anesthesia is thus maintained.

Another homemade variation useful to anesthetize small animals including rabbits is described by Dudley *et al.* (1975). The reader is referred to the original paper.

Methoxyflurane is effective following intravenous injection of thiopental. Methoxyflurane is then satisfactory at 3%, in a closed rebreathing system. Because of low vapor pressure at ordinary temperature (25 torr at

20° C), it is feasible to use methoxyflurane in a face cone, although in a well-ventilated room for operator protection. We find it to be very satisfactory in a face cone following sodium pentobarbital injection. Classic eye signs are useless to ascertain stages of anesthesia with methoxyflurane. In deep anesthesia such signs as lowered respiratory rate, muscle relaxation, and changes in pulse rate and degree of reflex activity are utilized.

c. *Ketamine Hydrochloride plus Methoxyflurane.* The use of a pre-anesthetic, e.g., 15 to 20 mg/kg of ketamine injected intravenously, has been advocated to facilitate intubation which then allows closed circuit administration of methoxyflurane (Lindquist, 1972). The endotracheal tube recommended by these authors is clear plastic of 3 mm I.D. and it has an external cuff. It is attachable to an anesthetic machine by a necked-down connector. The procedure is claimed to circumvent the tendency of the rabbit to hold its breath on inhaling the methoxyflurane vapors.

This procedure has been simplified (Wass, *et al.*, 1974). These authors state that no difficulty arises in administering methoxyflurane by nasal cone within 5 minutes after the intramuscular injection of ketamine in a dose of 44–55 mg/kg.

d. *Cyclopropane-Halothane.* A closed-circuit method is described for the administration of cyclopropane–oxygen and halothane–oxygen to rabbits (Watson, and Cowie, 1966). Preanesthesia is undertaken with intravenous injection of a short-acting barbiturate. This is followed by insertion of a laryngoscope through which an endotracheal tube is passed.

Cyclopropane is a gas which should be administered only in a closed system. Its mixtures with oxygen or air are flammable and explosive. The depth of anesthesia is best evaluated by depression of respiratory movements.

e. *Acepromazine-Methoxyflurane.* This mixture is claimed to provide adequate anesthesia for rabbits (McCormick, and Ashworth, 1971).

Acepromazine maleate (Atravet, Ayerst Labs., Montreal, Canada) is available in a concentration of 25 mg/ml. Dilute this with 10 times its volume of sterile water to produce a final concentration of 2.5 mg/ml. Inject into the paraspinal muscles 0.01 ml (equals 0.025 mg) for every 25 gm body weight. Use a tuberculin syringe graduated in 0.01 ml. Follow this in 60–90 minutes with inhalation of methoxyflurane, by wetting gauze with this drug and placing the gauze in the narrow end of a nasal cone. Do not wet the gauze excessively. Although the use of a closed circuit apparatus is preferable, it requires intubation with its attendant difficulties in the rabbit.

3. Anesthesia by Injection

In the usual procedures, anesthetics are introduced by injection into the body. The *intravenous* route in the rabbit is most convenient via the central or marginal veins of the ear. Direct the needle toward the heart. In all cases inject the anesthetic very slowly while watching the animal carefully. It is better to give less of the primary anesthetic and maintain a waiting policy before adding the remainder of the computed dose. In using barbiturates, we often underanesthetize and then supplement the barbiturate with a volatile liquid anesthetic by nasal cone. In using a single drug I.V., administer the anesthetic to effect and use the calculated dose only as a guide.

Some factors that influence the anesthetic responses are:

1. Excited and frightened animals often require a larger anesthetic dose for induction. This increased dose may produce an unexpectedly sudden effect such that the animal goes into respiratory paralysis.

2. Barbiturates can cause laryngospasm and bronchospasm. The rabbit appears to be emerging from surgical anesthesia, but dies in a few minutes. This can be prevented by tracheal intubation plus the administration of atropine just prior to anesthetizing the animal.

3. Extravascular injections of barbiturates can produce local tissue necrosis. If this occurs, infiltrate the area with 1% procaine (hydrochloride). Extravascular barbiturates are also slowly released into the system and can prolong or deepen the stage of anesthesia.

4. Very old and very young rabbits require a different anesthetic dose than does the young adult rabbit. Obesity, nutritional condition, and general health status can also affect the responses of rabbits to anesthetics.

The *intramuscular* route is preferably via the lateral aspect of the hindquarters. *Intraperitoneal* injection is made lateral to the midline, cranial to the vertex of the urinary bladder, and caudal to the stomach and liver.

a. Morphine. The major pharmacologic effect of this agent is analgesia. Give morphine subcutaneously, or intramuscularly into the back muscles of the lumbar region, 8 mg/kg. Morphine is not generally useful in the rabbit. When used as a preanesthetic, it can be followed by the barbiturates (especially sodium pentobarbital) or by ether inhalation.

There are narcotic antagonists useful for reversing the respiratory depression caused by morphine and related narcotics. The antagonists are specific for narcotics and do not restore respiration to normalcy in depression caused by barbiturates or other anesthetics. These specific antagonists include time-tested analeptics such as nalorphine hydrochloride, levallorphan tartrate, naloxone hydrochloride, and diprenorphine.

b. Sodium Pentobarbital. Inject the solution intravenously, very slowly into a vein of the ear, or sometimes through the jugular vein in operated rabbits where the neck region has been exposed. The drug is also effective intraperitoneally, and this route is one of choice if the ear veins cannot be injected.

The exact dose of sodium pentobarbital, especially for the New Zealand white rabbit, has not been definitely established, but it ranges from 30 to 60 mg/kg. We often use a 5% solution, in which 1 ml contains 50 mg. A different breed of rabbit may respond in a dissimilar way to the same dosage. If the dose does not produce deep anesthesia, use an inhalant anesthetic in a nose cone. We find methoxyflurane to be superior to ether in maintaining a smooth, deep stage.

Dolowy and Hesse (1959) recommend 25–100 mg/kg of chlorpromazine hydrochloride intramuscularly in the thighs. They follow this in 30 minutes by injecting into an ear vein 20 mg/kg of 3% sodium pentobarbital freshly dissolved in 10% alcohol. The tranquilizer facilitates induction of anesthesia and prolongs it, but there is the difficulty of combating an overdosage.

Sodium pentobarbital depresses respiration, but it has little effect upon blood pressure. One antidote for overdosage is 1 mg of picrotoxin/9 mg of pentobarbital.

The ultrashort-acting barbiturates, sodium evipan and sodium pentothal, are also useful in the rabbit. Surital (thiamyl sodium, Parke-Davis and Co.) is claimed to be an especially effective member of this group (Gardner, 1964). Give Surital i.v. in 1% solution, 31.5 mg/kg, very slowly. Induction time is about 3 minutes, deep anesthesia is 8.5 minutes, and recovery time is 5 to 15 minutes thereafter. Atropine is a useful preanesthetic agent to reduce the salivation that could obstruct the trachea.

c. Fentanyl and Droperidol (Innovar-Vet, McNeill Laboratories, Fort Washington, Pennsylvania). Inject intramuscularly 0.22 ml/kg of Innovar-Vet. Ether can be administered adjunctively by nose cone. The induction time in white rabbits is about 12 minutes and the duration of

deep anesthesia is from 45 to 105 minutes. Atropine alleviates the
bradycardia associated with the primary anesthetic mixture (see Strack
and Kaplan, 1968).

   *d. Propriopromazine Hydrochloride plus Paraldehyde plus Equi-
Thesin.* This combination has been described as being effective (Hodesson
et al., 1965). In following this procedure, inject intramuscularly (into the
dorsal aspect of the thigh) 5 mg/kg of propriopromazine plus 0.3 ml/kg of
paraldehyde. Follow this 45 minutes later by an intravenous marginal
ear vein injection of 2.5 ml/kg of Equi-Thesin.

   If the premedication is a mixture of 10 mg/kg of diazepam and 0.3
ml/kg of paraldehyde, the i.v. administration of Equi-Thesin is also
usually effective.

   Equi-Thesin (Jensen-Salsberry Labs., Kansas City, MO) is a combination of chloral hydrate, magnesium sulfate, sodium pentobarbital, pro-
pylene glycol, and alcohol.

   e. Paraldehyde. Inject undiluted paraldehyde, U.S.P., intraperitoneally with a 23-gauge needle. An assistant immobilizes the rabbit in
dorsal recumbency with its feet at 60° to the table top; this is to avoid
puncture of the visceral organs. As an additional precaution, withdraw
the syringe plunger slightly prior to injection to assure that the needle has
not punctured a blood vessel.

   A dose of 1.0–1.25 ml/kg produces deep anesthesia in 30–45 minutes
for a duration of 1–2 hours. Keep the animals warm and occasionally
rotated prior to their arousal within 3 to 8 hours (AALAS Newsletter
communication from Paul B. Steingruby, St. Louis).

   Paraldehyde can be a very irritating fluid and some workers use only
deep intramuscular injection, making this drug impossible for use in immature rabbits. The drug has a wide margin of safety in hypnotic doses
since it depresses the cerebrum but not the medullary center.

   f. Magnesium Sulfate. Give 4.0 ml of a 25% aqueous solution intraperitoneally. If the surgical plane of anesthesia is not attained, inject
another 2.0 ml after 10 minutes. Some investigators increase this dose
considerably, that is, 1.5 mg/kg, or 6 ml/kg of a 25% solution. Inject intravenously 8 ml of a 3% solution of calcium chloride or calcium
gluconate to overcome any respiratory depression that is produced by
magnesium sulfate.

   g. Urethane (Ethyl Carbamate). To obtain manageable volumes,
make up a 20% solution in 0.9% sodium chloride solution. Inject into the

marginal ear vein 1.5 mg/kg, slowly (Bree and Cohen, 1965). An intravenous dose of 2.0 gm/kg is lethal for rabbits.

Urethane can adversely affect blood and vessels. The superficial vessels can become greatly dilated. Hemolysis of blood may occur up to a few hours after injection. Blood clotting time greatly increases for a few hours.

Urethane provides stable anesthesia for 5–6 hours. It has a wider margin of safety than does sodium pentobarbital.

h. Ketamine Hydrochloride Alone. Intramuscular injections of 44 mg/kg of ketamine alone are stated to produce surgical anesthesia if only 15–25 minutes of operating time are needed (Weisbroth and Fudens, 1972. Induction time is 8–10 minutes. Recovery is complete 30–45 minutes after injection.

3. Oral Anesthesia

a. Paraldehyde. This is a useful analgesic by the oral route. Give it by stomach tube in a dose of 1 ml/kg.

b. Urethane. Give by stomach tube 1.8 gm/kg (9 ml of a 20% solution per kilogram). This can be followed 1 hour later by ether if needed, or, use an initial dose of 5 ml of a 20% aqueous solution (containing 1 gm/kg), followed by an intermediate dose of 0.6 gm/kg, if after the initial dose the corneal reflex is still obtainable. The animal must be kept warm when using urethane.

A useful rabbit stomach tube is a No. 12 French catheter (4 mm O. D.). A unit on the French scale is 1/3 mm. Thus, a No. 30 French catheter is 10 mm in diameter. Adapt the stem of a funnel to one end and dip the other end in glycerine. Introduce the catheter through a hole in a wooden mouth gag held between the upper and lower teeth. Avoid placing the catheter into the trachea.

4. Differentiation of Anesthesia from Asphyxia

Many of the signs of anesthesia and asphyxia are similar because the effect is to impair the function of the brain. Asphyxia implies that the brain has insufficient oxygen. Anesthesia implies a loss of sensory function and motor control, even in the presence of adequate oxygen.

5. Muscle Relaxants

Muscle relaxants are drugs used supplementary to the primary anesthetic agent to bring about better muscle relaxation.

The relaxants produce a predictable series of reactions. The muscles are affected in the following time sequence, first to last: face, jaw, tail, neck, limb, swallowing, phonatory, abdominal, intercostal, and diaphragm. The untreated rabbit will die of respiratory failure when an overdose is administered. Oxygen should always be available.

Most of the muscle relaxants effect their action at the myoneural junction. There are a number of these drugs. Succinylcholine and D-tubocurarine chloride are among those used commonly in physiologic experimentation.

Part II Laboratory Procedures Using the Rabbit

Chapter *4* General Mammalian Physiology and Surgical Techniques

Exercise 1 **Surgical Anatomy: Cervical Structures**

Two exercises have been designed to familiarize the worker with selected anatomic regions of the rabbit, and to help locate certain nerves, blood vessels, glands, and organs that will be involved in later exercises.

A. ANATOMY OF THE VENTRAL SURFACE OF THE NECK

Euthanatize a rabbit by overanesthesia and secure it to a surgical table with its ventral surface upward. This position of the animal is called dorsal recumbency, or supine. Using scissors and a depilatory solution, remove an area of hair approximately 6 cm wide and extending from the angle of the mandible to the proximal end of the sternum.

Taking care to keep the head and neck in a straight line, palpate the trachea and incise 6 or 7 cm along the midline through the skin, superficial muscles, and fascia. Reflect the skin laterally with tissue forceps and clear away all connective tissue.

Locate and identify the following structures and note their anatomic relationships (Fig. 14):

The *ribbon muscles* lie on the ventral surface of the trachea. The paired sternohyoids are on either side of the midline. Observe the deeper sternothyroids and the more lateral omohyoids. The thyrohyoids lie more cranially.

The *trachea* lies along the midline, and can best be identified by the cartilaginous tracheal rings that support it.

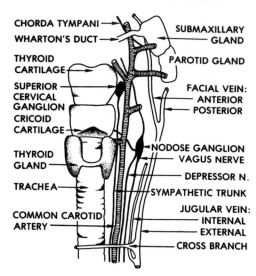

Figure 14.   Neck anatomy. Major structures seen in ventral dissection of the neck. Superficial structures have been removed.

The *cricoid cartilage* is a thick, annular cartilage located just above the first tracheal ring.

The *thyroid cartilage* of the larynx is saddle-shaped. It lies just cranial to the cricoid cartilage and is connected by the cricothyroid ligament and muscle.

The *thyroid gland* is composed of two lobes, a right and a left, the two being connected by a thin portion, the isthmus. The gland lies ventral and lateral to the trachea at the level of the cricoid cartilage.

The *common carotid artery* runs parallel and lateral to the trachea. It is surrounded by the carotid sheath, which should be cleared away. Trace the artery superiorly and locate first the *superior thyroid* artery and the *laryngeal* artery, both of which branch from the common carotid.

The *internal jugular* vein lies parallel to the trachea and lateral to the common carotid artery.

The *external jugular* vein is larger than, and lies superficial to, the internal jugular. In the dead animal the veins can be distinguished by the thinness of their walls, as compared to the thicker, whiter, arterial walls.

The *vagus nerve* lies between the common carotid artery and the internal jugular vein. The vagus is usually the largest of the nerves accompanying the common carotid artery.

The *cervical sympathetic trunk* is medial to the vagus and lies on the dorsal surface of the common carotid artery. Stimulation in the live rabbit of the cervical sympathetic trunk will induce vasoconstriction that is visible in the blood vessels of the ear.

The *superior cervical ganglion* is located by tracing the sympathetic trunk cranially from the cricoid cartilage. The ganglion lies medial to both the vagus nerve and the internal carotid artery.

The *depressor nerve* lies on the dorsal surface of the common carotid artery, medial to the cervical sympathetic trunk. The depressor nerve is usually the smallest nerve accompanying the common carotid artery.

The *superior* and *inferior laryngeal nerves* are paired branches of the vagus trunk. The superior pair leave the main trunk at the level of the cranial border of the thyroid cartilage, and pass medially into the laryngeal structures. The inferior pair pass cranially into the larynx from below the thyroid cartilage.

B. AIRWAY AND VESSEL CANNULATION

In rabbits being dissected anatomically for visualization of structures of later surgical interest, it is expedient to practice cannulation of airways and blood vessels. The following descriptions are for procedures that will be used in some subsequent exercises on live, anesthetized rabbits.

C. INSERTION OF A TRACHEAL CANNULA

With curved forceps slip two ligatures under the exposed trachea. Lift the organ and make a ventral T-shaped incision in its wall. Insert a

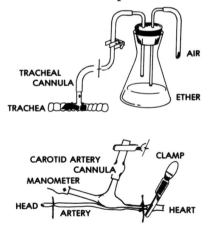

Figure 15. Cannulas. Insertion of tracheal and arterial cannulas. Upper figure: cannula inserted into trachea. Lower figure: cannula inserted into carotid artery in the classic manometric procedure.

tracheal cannula pointing toward the lungs and tie it securely in place with the ligatures. Connect it by rubber tubing to a bottle such as an Erlenmeyer flask containing absorbent cotton saturated with an inhalant anesthetic. The flask should possess a 2-hole stopper with 2 glass tubes running through it, one as an inlet for air and the other as an outlet for the anesthetic-air mixture. The mixture can be regulated by partially closing the inlet side with a Hoffman clamp. This allows maintained anesthesia if necessary. The tracheostomy also permits use of apparatus for artificial respiration. This assembly will be found useful in later work with live, anesthetized rabbits. Its use in the present exercise is only to familiarize the student with its arrangement in desirable manipulative processes (Fig. 15).

A suitable tracheal cannula is a commercially available cannula for cats, sizes "small" or "very small" (Harvard Apparatus Co., Millis, Massachusetts).

D. INSERTION OF AN ENDOTRACHEAL CATHETER

The passage of a cuffed endotracheal catheter through the mouth can be performed in the rabbit, but with considerable difficulty since the glottis is narrow and the larynx is not easily seen because of the shape of the tongue. An internal catheter bore of 3.0–3.5 mm is in the range of usefulness.

Attempt the following procedure. Squeeze the cheeks of the rabbit between the upper and lower teeth with your thumb and index finger to open the animal's mouth and grasp the tongue with a gauze sponge. Use a laryngoscope with a Moore premature infant blade. Introduce the blade and push the catheter into the trachea. Substitute a straight pediatric blade for large rabbits. Practice this in the euthanatized rabbit. In later experiments with live rabbits, work with the animal under anesthesia.

A procedure has been described in which a rabbit can be sedated with an ultrashort-acting barbiturate, a laryngoscope inserted, and a polyvinyl chloride endotracheal tube (I.D. 3.0 mm) passed through the laryngoscope (Watson and Cowie, 1966).

An oral speculum facilitating intubation has been devised (Hoge *et al.*, 1969). The authors describe its use in an anesthetized rabbit as follows.

Pry the mouth open and position a speculum behind the upper and lower incisor teeth. With the tongue pulled forward and laterally with a smooth clamp, advance an endotracheal tube past the resisting epiglottis and into the trachea. Use semirigid plastic tubing about 4 inches long, the size of a No. 17 French cuffless catheter, and slightly curved with a pointed end. If difficulty is encountered in passage in later work on live rabbits, spray a topical anesthetic into the throat. The endotracheal tube permits linkage to an anesthetic machine for administration of drugs such as methoxyflurane or halothane. Practice this procedure in the anatomically dissected rabbit.

E. CANNULATION OF THE CAROTID ARTERY

If the neck of the euthanatized rabbit has been anatomically exposed, as described above, then directly cannulate the carotid artery with polyethylene tubing to gain practice in passing such tubes.

Because later work involves live, anesthetized rabbits, directions follow which will be found useful when anesthesia has been mastered and the animal is operated upon so that the carotid artery is exposed in the surgically dissected neck and a cannula is inserted into the pulsating vessel.

In the rabbit under surgical anesthesia (later exercises) incise along the midline from the caudal end of the larynx to the suprasternal notch. Use blunt dissection in all further procedures. Separate the muscles ventral to the trachea. With hemostats, separate the sternomastoid from the sternothyroid muscle. Between these, in a groove lateral to the trachea, observe the common carotid artery pulsating within a heavy sheath.

Separate the fascia from the carotid sheath so that it lies free for at least 1½ inches. Open the sheath to expose the artery that is accompanied by the vagus nerve and the internal jugular vein. Use a mosquito (fine-lipped) forceps in these dissections to prevent tearing. Separate all structures within the sheath by clearing away the fascia. In the anatomically dissected rabbit the cervical sympathetic trunk should have been seen as a distinct structure in the sheath.

Ligate the cephalic portion of the artery, leaving long ligature ends. Compress the artery on the portion toward the heart. For compression, use a bulldog clamp to minimize crushing forces or else cover the tips of light hemostats with rubber tubing. Between the two constricted areas pass a third, loosely placed ligature under the artery. Pull on the cephalic ligature while nicking the vessel just below it. Use a scissors to make a V-shaped cut. The points of the scissors are directed toward the heart. If the blood flows, it indicates that the vessel has been entered. Insert a cannula into the V-shaped cut and direct it toward the heart. Fix it firmly with the middle ligature and reinforce this binding with the long ends of the cephalic ligature.

Polyethylene tubing (PE–90 is of proper diameter (I.D. 0.86 mm or 0.034 inches) to cannulate the blood vessel. A No. 25 needle is satisfactory for injection of fluids into the rabbit vessels.

In a later exercise, when taking end blood pressures for recording, connect the free end of the cannula, in the classic system, by pressure tubing to a U-tube manometer containing mercury. In the more acceptable modern method of taking blood pressures in the operated animal, connect electronic transduction devices in series with an inserted polyethylene catheter.

Exercise 2   Surgical Anatomy: Abdomen, Blood Vessels, and Nerves

A. VISCERAL ORGANS OF THE ABDOMINAL CAVITY

Euthanatize a rabbit by overanesthesia and secure it to a surgical table with its ventral side up. Make a median incision through the skin only, extending from the xiphoid process to the pubic symphysis. Retract the skin and then dissect clean the underlying fascia.

The median aponeurotic line (midline) that extends from the xiphoid process to the pubic symphysis is the linea alba. Make a longitudinal incision along this plane to open the peritoneal cavity and expose the abdominal viscera.

Identify the following structures (Fig. 16). Observe their positions. Trace their major blood vessels and nerves.

The *stomach* is caudal to the esophagus. Observe the cardiac end, the main body of the stomach, and the pylorus, or region of junction with the intestines.

The *duodenum* forms a U-shaped loop that is situated on the dorsal abdominal wall.

The *jejunum* and *ileum* are the succeeding portions of the small intestine. They are not readily separable in external view.

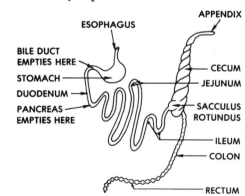

Figure 16. Intestinal tract. Diagram of isolated alimentary canal.

The *cecum* is of considerable size. It is the entrance section of the large intestine.

The *colon* is the major part of the large intestine. It is divided into ascending, transverse, and descending parts.

The *pancreas* lies dorsal and caudal to the stomach. Unlike the situation in man, the pancreatic duct empties into the small intestine independently of the bile duct from the liver.

The *liver* is partially divided into right and left lobes. The *gallbladder,* or reservoir for the liver bile, is situated on the dorsal surface of the right lobe of the liver.

The *common bile duct* is formed on the dorsal surface of the liver by union of the hepatic ducts from the lobes of the liver. The common bile duct receives the cystic duct of the gallbladder. The combined duct system penetrates the dorsal surface of the first part of the duodenum just caudal to the pylorus.

The student should attempt to place a cannula into the common bile duct. He should also note the positions of the cystic artery and vein, so that he can tie them off during later surgery of the biliary tracts.

The *kidneys* lie on the dorsal wall of the cavity and can be easily identified if the intestines are moved aside (Fig. 17).

The *ureter* can be seen behind the peritoneum as a white tube passing backward from the hilus of the kidney into the dorsal portion of the urinary bladder.

The *urinary bladder* is a thin-walled muscular sac lying in the ventral pelvic portion of the abdominal cavity.

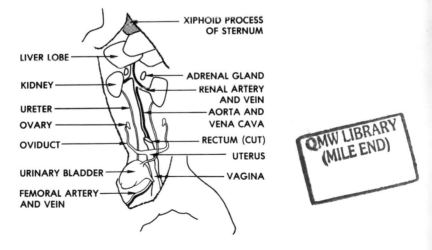

Figure 17. Abdominal anatomy. Abdominal structures seen in diagrammatic view after removing the digestive organs.

The *urethra* is a structure running caudally from the bladder and it empties in the floor of the vagina which connects to the exterior of the body. Attempt to pass a cannula into the urethra and on into the urinary bladder.

The *adrenal glands* are small paired structures that lie a short distance medial to the cranial end of each kidney.

Observe the following in a female rabbit:

The *ovary* is a small elongated structure on the dorsal body wall, a short distance caudal to the kidney.

The *uterine tube* is the first portion of the oviduct. Its very narrow upper end broadens to a funnellike receptacle where it opens into the peritoneal cavity.

The *uterus* is the second portion of the oviduct, characterized by its greater diameter and muscular walls. The right and left horns of the uterus fuse together and form the body of the uterus. The uterus is continuous distally with the vagina (Fig. 18).

B. THE FEMORAL ARTERY, VEIN, AND NERVE

Make a small vertical incision in the uppermost part of the ventral thigh; remove the skin as well as any fascia and connective tissue, and expose the femoral artery, vein, and nerve. The vein is occasionally used for withdrawal of blood or for injection of solutions (Fig. 19).

C. THE SCIATIC NERVE

Expose the whole length of the nerve from the sciatic notch to the ankle by reflecting the biceps muscle and turning aside the lateral head of the

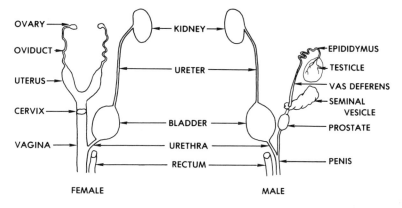

Figure 18.   Urogenital organs. Comparison of female and male urogenital structures.

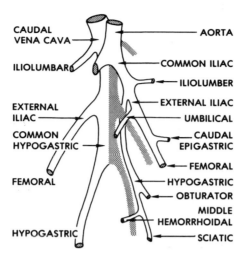

Figure 19. Major pelvic blood vessels. All captions on the left refer to venous tributaries of the caudal (inferior) vena cava. All those on the right refer to arterial branches of the abdominal aorta.

gastrocnemius after cutting through it close to the bone. The blood vessels cut in this approach are cutaneous vessels, the saphenous vein, and the muscular branches of the biceps and gastrocnemius muscles.

The sciatic nerve is formed chiefly from the last lumbar and first sacral nerves (Fig. 20). It is seen laterally in the great sciatic notch. It passes dorsally beneath the piriform muscle and then travels distally to the thigh, where it lies on the lateral surfaces of the adductors magnus and

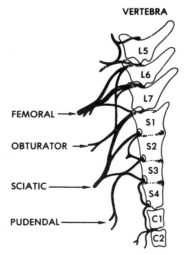

Figure 20. Lumbosacral plexus. Diagram of nerves forming lumbosacral plexus.

longus. It distributes branches to the dorsal muscles of the thigh. In the proximal portion, the nerve divides to two main branches that are closely associated down to the knee; the ventral branch is the peroneal nerve and the dorsal branch is the tibial nerve. Just above the knee joint the tibial branch produces the small saphenous nerve.

Other nerves in the hindlimb should be examined after dissecting the sciatic nerve. The femoral nerve is important and it originates chiefly from the fifth lumbar segment of the lumbosacral plexus. Just distal to the inguinal ligament it splits to two. One branch innervates the ventral muscles of the thigh. The other, which is the great saphenous nerve, travels to the medial surface of the thigh and leg, at first with the femoral artery and then with the great saphenous artery.

Exercise 3   **Ether Anesthesia**

Although the use of ether* has been markedly decreasing, and with ample cause, it is an anesthetic which sharply brings into focus for the beginner the stages of anesthesia, and it is one in which resuscitation is within fairly effective control. It is with this in mind that we devote a laboratory exercise to the observation of behavior and vital signs of rabbits subjected to ether first by a cone covering the nose and mouth, followed by vapors of the drug introduced into the airways through a tracheal cannula.

Ether depresses the central nervous system. Excess etherization causes failure of the respiratory center. There is an effect upon circulatory dynamics in that subsequent lack of oxygen injures the heart, slowing it and dropping the blood pressure.

For all animals to be anesthetized, construct a chart which includes observations on respiration, pulse, carotid blood pressure where feasible, rectal temperature, width of the pupils, voluntary movements, muscle tone, pedal reflex, corneal reflex, and any other pertinent data. Review anesthesia in Chapter 3. The following numerical values illustrate what to expect:

1. The respiratory rate in a conscious rabbit being handled is considerably above the basal rate and averages about 160/minute. This falls during etherization. At 40/minute discontinue the anesthesia until "normalcy" is resumed.

2. The heart rate in a conscious rabbit being handled is about 180/minute. Take the count by placing the fingertips over the intercostal spaces or use a stethoscope. Light anesthesia increases the rate sharply. During respiratory collapse the rate falls abruptly.

3. The mean arterial blood pressure taken via a transducer from the

*Note that ether is explosive!.

carotid artery in the anesthetized rabbit is 90–100 torr. Discontinue the etherization if the pressure falls below 80.

4. The average normal rectal temperature is 103.1°F (about 40°C) with a range of 101.5°–104.2°F. A drop of a few degrees is to be expected during the first hour of etherization.

Etherize first through a nose cone, and then through an ether bottle connected to the tracheal cannula. Maintain an even anesthesia, applying the cone lightly to allow oxygen entrance. Observe the disappearance of voluntary movements; the relaxation of muscle tone; reflex loss, the last to go being the corneal reflex; and the shrinking in the size of the pupil.

Stage I. Analgesia. The first stage, impaired consciousness, is brief. The animal is drowsy.

Stage II. Excitement. The second stage is one of excitement. Movements are wild. The pupils dilate and salivation is copious. The animal struggles to escape. The pulse and respiratory rate increase.

Stage III. Surgical anesthesia. The third stage is one of surgical anesthesia. Spontaneous movements disappear. The heart rate and respiratory rates are normal. Limb reflexes are gone but the corneal reflex persists. Draw a bit of cotton over the cornea without touching the lids, and the animal winks. Keep the animal in this stage if anesthesia is to be maintained for a long time.

Stage IV. Respiratory arrest (medullary). In the fourth stage, anesthesia is excessively deep. Reflexes disappear. The pupils dilate widely. Sphincters relax. The pulse and respiratory rate fall. The red color of the lips fades or changes. The forelimbs extend and the chest enlarges. The muscles have a nonresisting flabbiness. In Stage III, they are firm. Determine by palpating the large muscles of the legs.

If artificial respiration is given, uncover the lateral opening in the tracheal cannula to allow escape of expired air. If the lungs expand, clean mucus out of the cannula.

If the animal dies prematurely, assume the cause to be improper anesthesia. Perform a necropsy to determine other causes.

Some rabbits make continual swallowing movements during ether anesthesia. This is evidence of faulty administration of ether. It may be given too fast or in excess amounts so that condensation occurs, producing irritation of the mucous membranes of the respiratory tract. Placing too much ether into the gauze is a common fault. Watch for evidence of this, such as continual gurgling sounds and chewing movements.

We advise the supplementary use of ether or other inhalant anesthetics in subsequent exercises if deep anesthesia has not been attained by sodium pentobarbital alone. The tendency of the beginner to continue to inject barbiturate increases the danger of asphyxia. We also emphasize the fact that rabbits tend to hold their breath in the initial stages of use of ether when it is used as the primary anesthetic, leading the operator to overly aggressive application of the ether cone.

The person designated as anesthetist should maintain his attention to the application of the ether cone and to any signs of faulty administration throughout the exercise. Walking away from the animal will lead to disaster.

Exercise 4   Absorption of Anesthetics by the Large Intestine

The large intestine is capable of limited absorption, including the absorption of gases. The possibility of anesthesia using volatile drugs by the rectal route may be explored and the efficiency compared with that of the more acceptable method of inhalation. This is an old experiment in the literature.

Set an ether bottle, carrying a cork stopper with two glass tubes, into a water bath at 40°C. This temperature is just above the boiling point of ether. Insert one tube, previously coated with vaseline, mineral oil, or soap, into the rectum. Air will be sucked into the bottle from the vent in the other tube, and ether may be vaporized rapidly into the rectum by the occasional manual compression of a rubber bulb inserted at will over the air vent.

Observe the temporal appearance of the usual bodily signs of ether anesthesia. How long does it take for the breath to smell of ether? After what time do muscle reflexes disappear?

With the rabbit lying on an animal table, take recordings, at 5-minute intervals for at least 1 hour of the heart rate, respiratory rate, rectal temperature, pupillary diameter, reflex activity, and muscle tonus. What care must be taken during operative procedures upon the rabbit?

EFFICIENCIES OF PARENTAL METHODS

Compare the efficiency of morphine with ether. Also, compare the results of subcutaneous and intramuscular injections of morphine. Give morphine sulfate, 10 mg/kg, subcutaneously to one animal and intramuscularly through the dorsal lumbar muscles to another. Observe in each rabbit the activity, muscle tone, heart rate, respiratory rate, and rectal temperature, at 5-minute intervals, for 1 hour. Write up your conclusions. Would you use morphine for anesthesia or for preanesthesia?

Exercise 5   **Spinal Anesthesia**

The rabbit has a highly adaptable structure for a subarachnoid injection (Bieter *et al.*, 1936). The injection is made through a large intervertebral space at the lumbosacral junction. This opening is approximately 0.5 cm in diameter in a 2-kg animal. The filum terminale is beneath it. Since any significant amount of spinal fluid is unavailable by spinal puncture, the effects of injected drugs may be observed in concentrations that do not become diluted.

Gray chinchilla rabbits have more uniform bony landmarks than other varieties but the white rabbit is satisfactory. Place the rabbit in a canvas hammock, with the animal's legs extending downward through four properly spaced holes. This position flattens the spinal curves, and an almost horizontal line may be drawn from the center of the head to the sacrum.

The anesthetic dose is determined on a basis of spinal length. Measure the length by pressing the end of a steel tape both ventrally and cranially against the occiput when the head is sharply flexed, carrying the tape over the spine, following its curves, and ending over the upper and most prominent sacral spinous process.

To decrease struggling and to arch the back, tie the forelegs closely to the hind legs. This separates the vertebral spines and permits easier entrance of the needle. Use a tuberculin syringe with a 22-gauge needle.

The injection site is located. Rest your left forearm on the rabbit's back. Place the left thumb and middle finger on the iliac crests. The index finger can touch the last lumbar vertebra that is on a line between the crests. Move the index finger caudally to locate the first sacral spine. The injection space is in the lumbo–sacral junction between these two spines.

With the right hand place the needle with the bevel downward just lateral to the cranial end of the first sacral process. Hold it at about 45° (forward) to the spinal axis during needle insertion and injection into the subarachnoid space. The needle is inserted off the midline, with the purpose of its reaching the midline when piercing the dura.

The needle pierces a tough skin, a softer muscle, a dense and resistant ligamentum flava, and finally a soft dura and arachnoid, and the "give" through the ligamentum flava is an index of entrance into the subarachnoid space. Aspirate the syringe; if blood is withdrawn, the needle has overpenetrated the cord and has entered a ventral blood vessel.

Using moderate pressure with the left forearm on the rabbit's back, inject at a rate not exceeding 1–2 ml/minute. A dose of 0.02 ml/cm of spinal length provides sufficient fluid practically to fill the subarachnoid space throughout the spinal cord.

An important sign of anesthetic depression following any route of drug application is the effect upon respiration. Apply strong electrical stimuli with an electronic stimulator to the skin of an unanesthetized rabbit. Observe the heightened respiratory movements. Note on the stimulator the minimal values necessary to obtain the respiratory changes. In later trials with the anesthetic you used, observe whether similar respiratory changes occur at the same threshold settings of the stimulator.

All solutions to be injected spinally should be sterile. Begin with an injection of 0.9% sodium chloride. Note any adverse reactions such as fine tremors of the abdomen and limbs, or else spastic contractions of the limbs.

Produce spinal anesthesia with several drugs, each rabbit tested receiving only one drug. Try 2.0% procaine hydrochloride, 0.08% Nupercaine, and any other. Evaluate the progress of anesthesia in each case.

Compare the spinal method with ether inhalation. Spinal anesthesia may not control responses from such visceral organs as the esophagus, liver, and stomach. Vagal and phrenic impulses are not blocked. Use appropriate stimuli in attempting to elicit responses.

Death from respiratory failure is a danger. A permanent motor paralysis is another danger.

If desired, visualize the respiratory rhythm, force, and frequency by pneumography. In the classic method an animal pneumograph strapped around the chest is connected by pressure tubing to a Marey tambour which writes a record of respiratory excursions on a moving drum. The much improved electronic method uses (1) a pressure transducer with an attached flexible bellows strapped around the chest, or (2) an impedance pneumograph. The impedance penumograph is a transducer/preamplifier, requiring only that two needle, disk, or plate electrodes be attached to the chest. A current of about 2 microamperes is passed through the attached electrodes. The voltage across the electrodes is directly proportional to the animal's chest impedance. Small voltage variations produced by the impedance changes are amplified and detected as a signal for recording on a channel recorder. Satisfactory bellows pneumographs or impedance pneumographs for student work are commercially available (one type used here being the system from Narco Bio-Systems, Houston, Texas 77017).

Exercise 6   **Laparotomy**

Students can be introduced to their first rabbit survival surgery simply by undertaking to perform an abdominal incision, or laparotomy, under sterile conditions. The wound is sutured and the animal is held postsurgically in a recovery room and allowed to return under both staff and student supervision to a fully healed state. The student is thus made to learn and apply the knowledge and principles of anesthesia, surgery, and aftercare which are fundamental to all surgery. Exercises with the rabbit which increase the manipulative skill of the student can be emphasized either in a designated course in experimental animal surgery, or else interspersed as in this text with classic exercises in mammalian physiology. The rabbit is a convenient animal for teaching surgical skills, since it is hardy, readily manageable, and esthetically acceptable to the student.

PROCEDURE

Anesthetize the rabbit with sodium pentobarbital given very slowly into an ear vein. Tie the animal in a supine position. Clip and shave the abdominal skin, then swab the area to be incised as well as the areas to the right and left of it in a peripheral direction with ethyl alcohol and then 2% iodine. Drape the abdomen and secure the drape to the skin with four towel clamps.

Make a paramedian incision with the scalpel and blade immediately lateral to the midline, starting about 5 cm (2 inches) below the xiphoid cartilage of the sternum and extending the incision 10 cm (4 inches) caudally. Cut only the skin and superficial fascia and make a firm bold incision in one passage. Use sponges and gauze to stop any minor bleeding. Use hemostats only if bleeding cannot be stopped. Tie off the clamped vessels with No. 00 surgical gut.

Dissect the superficial fascia with scissors having blunt–blunt ends and expose the deep fascia. Avoiding the rectus abdominis muscle, dissect longitudinally. After inserting a hemostat into the muscle, open the hemostat longitudinal to the muscle fibers, then use your fingers to pull the muscle fibers apart longitudinally along the length of the incision.

Cut the peritoneum along its length with scissors or scalpel, after elevating it with forceps to avoid puncturing underlying visceral organs. A groove director is helpful in orienting the incision. Gently explore the visceral organs with your fingers, noting their identity and geographic relationships.

Close the incision in reverse order. Lift the cut edges of the peritoneum with tissue forceps, approximate the edges, and using a half-circle needle held by a needle holder, close the wound with No. 00 medium chromic surgical gut. In small rabbits, close the peritoneum and muscle together.

Keep in mind the fact that the rabbit peritoneum is much more delicate than that of larger animals.

It is not necessary to close the ventral abdominal fascia in the rabbit. In the next step bring the skin edges together with simple interrupted sutures. Nonabsorbable suture is satisfactory, threaded on a half-circle needle. Do not approximate the opposing edges too tightly. Wrap a previously autoclaved bandage around the abdomen to prevent the rabbit when it awakens from tearing out the skin sutures. Do not bandage too tightly.

Remove the sutures 7–14 days later, depending upon the status of wound healing. Observe the rabbit frequently in the first week for gross behavior, general condition, and the appearance of the wound.

Exercise 7   Food Changes in the Digestive Tract

This is a highly simplified acute exercise to provide initial experience in observing internal structures in a live anesthetized rabbit and to develop teamwork. It requires a surgeon, anesthetist, and technician–recorder. Each group should construct a chart showing bodily changes during the course of anesthesia.

Feed a rabbit 60 minutes prior to the operative procedures. Arrange to include green vegetables as part of the meal.

Anesthetize the animal and open its abdomen. Use hemostats to control any bleeding.

Note the size of the distended stomach. Observe the peristaltic movements of the stomach and intestines.

Keep the intestines warm by applying gauze sponges dipped in warm Ringer's solution. Lift up a portion of the intestinal mesentery and note the circulation. The reddish arterial vessels are distinguishable from the more purplish veins. The main lymphatic vessel is found as a thin white structure between the most prominent artery and vein of the mesentery.

Expose 10 cm of the intestine near the pylorus. Squeeze out a sponge previously dipped in very hot Ringer's solution and place the sponge over the intestine. Remove the sponge and look for one or more somewhat violent peristaltic waves. Watch these waves traveling the length of the intestine.

Observe the gallbladder and its ducts. Is any activity evident?

With two mosquito forceps covered with rubber tubing, clamp off about 10 cm of the upper intestine. Inject enough saline solution to distend the clamped-off area. Keep this localized region warm with wet sponges. Watch the slow but gradual decrease in the distention of the intestine as the saline is absorbed. Remove the clamps.

Euthanatize the animal with an excess of the anesthetic. Remove the stomach by first clamping off the duodenum with two hemostats and cutting between them. Cut the stomach loose from the esophagus in the same manner.

Place the stomach on a tray and cut it open longitudinally. Watch the muscle tissue as it contracts when cut. Expose the gastric contents and observe the changes in consistency and color of these contents from the cardiac sphincter to the pylorus.

Filter the contents and obtain clear gastric juice. Test its pH with an electronic pH meter. Ascertain its free and total acidity.

Wash out the residual contents and view the stomach rugae. Stretch the stomach and pin it to a board. Note the decrease in the prominence of the folds occurring with stretch.

Remove the ileocecal valve, leaving about 10 cm of colon and ileum attached. Split the sphincter open and note the changes in the color and consistency of the contents on either side of the valve. Compare the contents of the colon with those of the stomach. Test its acidity with indicators. Wash out the colon and compare the appearance of its inner wall with that of the stomach.

TECHNICAL DIRECTIONS

Free and Total Acidity.

With a pipette transfer 5 ml of filtered gastric juice into a beaker. Add 3 drops of Topfer's reagent. This is a 0.5% alcoholic solution of dimethylaminoazobenzol. In the presence of free acid, a carmine-red color is immediately produced; otherwise the fluid turns canary-yellow. If red appears, titrate the fluid against 0.1 N NaOH from a burette. The end point is the appearance of the canary-yellow color. Note the milliliters of sodium hydroxide run in, and multiply by 20. This indicates the milliliters or "units" of free hydrocholoric acid present in 100 ml of gastric contents.

The gastric contents should be fresh, since free acid changes to combined acid on standing. Many workers filter the juice before titration. A suction filter is necessary if considerable mucus is present.

To find the total acidity, add 4 drops of 1% alcoholic phenolphthalein to the gastric juice in the beaker. Add 0.1 N NaOH from the burette until a rose-red color is reached that does not become deeper by adding another drop.

The total acidity is the amount of sodium hydroxide used in both titrations. Each milliliter of sodium hydroxide equals 0.00265 gm of hydrochloric acid, so that multiplying the milliliters of base used by this factor gives the percentage of hydrochloric acid.

The pH of rabbit gastric juice is approximately 1.6. The free acid is about 80 units, and the total acidity is about 105 units. All data should be converted to milliequivalents per liter, which has supplanted the awkward term "units" which refers to titration.

$$\text{mEq/liter} = \frac{\text{mg/100 x 10}}{\text{equivalent weight}}$$

Exercise 8   Fluid and Mineral Absorption in the Intestine

Deprive a rabbit of food for 24 hours and anesthetize it with sodium pentobarbital. Open the abdomen and tie off a loop of the small intestine with ligatures at least 24 cm apart. Make partial transverse incisions at each end of this loop and insert glass cannulae. Connect one cannula with a funnel and wash the loop out with warm 0.9% sodium chloride solution. Avoid any injury that might produce bleeding into the lumen of the intestine. Use large cannulae to obtain an easy flow.

Put in sufficient 0.9% sodium chloride solution warmed to 37° C to fill the loop without distention, measuring the volume required. See that the solution is all in the intestine; do not allow any of it to stand in the cannulae. Put the loop back with care to avoid kinking, and close the abdominal cavity with clamps. Keep the animal warm with dry warm towels covering the body. After 30 minutes allow the contents of the loop to run into a beaker, measure its volume and analyze the fluid for chloride content by any suitable chloride method. Measure the change in volume and the change in chloride concentration.

The exercise may be modified, if desired, to study the *rate* of absorption of chloride. In doing this, remove samples of the saline fluid in the isolated intestinal sac at carefully specified intervals and analyze each sample for its chloride concentration. Draw a graph relating the mineral absorption to time in minutes.

Euthanatize the rabbit by an overdose of the anesthetic.

TECHNICAL DIRECTIONS–CHLORIDE DETERMINATION

1. Theory

Determine choloride ions by titration with mercuric nitrate. The mercuric chloride is so little ionized that it does not react with the indicator, diphenylcarbazone. When an excess of mercuric ions is added, the reaction gives a blue-violet color with the indicator.

2. Reagents

a. Mercuric Nitrate. Dissolve 1.7 gm reagent-grade mercuric nitrate monohydrate and 2.6 ml concentrated nitric acid in 200 ml water. Dilute to 1 liter. This is stable in a brown glass bottle.

b. Indicator. Dissolve 100 mg s-diphenylcarbazone (Eastman Kodak Co., Rochester, New York) in 100 ml of 95% ethyl alcohol. Store in brown bottle in refrigerator.

c. Chloride Standard. Dry reagent grade sodium chloride at 120°C for several hours. Dissolve 584.5 mg of this in water to make 1 liter This solution contains 10 mEq/liter chloride.

3. Procedure.

Pipette 0.2 ml test fluid and 1.8 ml distilled water into an Erlenmeyer flask. Add 2 to 3 drops of indicator. The solution can be transferred to a small porcelain basin. The white background allows observation of the subsequent indicator change. Titrate with mercuric nitrate solution from a buret having a fine glass tip and calibrated in 0.01-ml intervals. Stir constantly with a glass rod bent like a hockey stick.

The clear solution becomes an intense violet upon addition of the first drop of mercuric nitrate. (If the titration is continued, the violet color may disappear to a pale pink with the violet color appearing again at the end point.) Use the first titration end point.

To standardize the mercuric nitrate solution, similarly titrate 0.2 ml of standard chloride solution (which was first pipetted into 1.8 ml water). Note that for deproteinization, if necessary, add to each of the two flasks above prior to titration 1 drop of $2/3\ N\ H_2SO_4$.

4. *Calculation.*

Since 2 ml of a 1:10 dilution and 2 ml of a 10 mEq/liter standard are titrated, this is equivalent to titrating 2 ml of an unknown test solution and 2 ml of a 100 mEq/liter standard. Thus:

$$\frac{\text{ml titration of test fluid}}{\text{ml titration of standard}} \times 100 = \text{mEq/liter of chloride}$$

To express chloride concentration in terms of mg/100 ml NaCl:

$$\text{mEq/liter chloride} \times 5.85 = \text{mg/100 ml sodium chloride}$$

Note that chloride ions in fluids can be measured more accurately by potentiometry. The autoanalyzer (Technicon, Chauncey, New York) measures chloride colorimetrically. The reason for a decline in the classic procedure of estimating chloride by titration is the difficulty of detecting the true end point.

Exercise 9   Neural Control of Esophageal, Gastric, and Intestinal Motility

Anesthetize a rabbit with an inhalation anesthetic and construct a chart showing the progress of anesthesia. Separate the trachea from the esophagus, avoiding injury to the nerves between these organs. Loop a thread under each vagus nerve. Isolate the superior laryngeal branch of the vagus nerve and pass a ligature under it; this nerve goes transversely across the neck and enters the side of the thyroid cartilage.

Insert a tracheal cannula very low in the neck and continue the anesthesia via this route. Remove the pieces of trachea between the cannula and the cricoid cartilage. The esophagus is brought into view. Note its texture and motility. Observe the thyroid gland and its blood supply and avoid bleeding from that source.

Open the mouth, touch the fauces with moist cotton, and note the swallowing movements. Stimulate with an electronic stimulator the central end of the superior laryngeal nerve. Results?

Expose the stomach and intestines. Observe the movements. Stimulate the small intestine mechanically and observe the myenteric reflex. Stimulate one vagus nerve with moderate tetanizing current from the stimulator. What is the effect on gastric peristalsis and intestinal movements? Cut the right vagus nerve in the neck and stimulate the superior laryngeal nerve. What difference is observed? What is the nervous mechanism of swallowing? Transect the esophagus and repeat the stimulation. Is the wave a series of reflexes or a muscular wave?

Make a small opening in the cardiac stomach and introduce a finger through the hole. Stimulate the superior laryngeal nerve and note the relaxation and tightening of the sphincter.

Since this is an acute procedure, the rabbit must be euthanatized with an overdose of the anesthetic.

Exercise 10   Secretion of Bile or Pancreatic Juice

The inexperienced operator often has difficulty in locating the pancreatic duct in the rabbit. Thus, this exercise is more suitable for manipulation of the bile duct, which can be more easily visualized and cannulated. Unlike the situation in man, the bile duct of the rabbit opens into the intestine several centimeters cranial to the pancreatic duct, as an independent tube.

Anesthetize a rabbit with sodium pentobarbital. Construct a chart of data to show the progress of anesthesia. Tie the animal down in supine position to the surgical table.

Expose one vagus nerve in the neck and place two ligatures loosely around the nerve, without tying the ligatures.

Open up the abdominal cavity by a ventral longitudinal incision and locate the duodenum. In one procedure, slit open the duodenum and locate the papilla which contains the opening of the common bile duct. Catheterize the duct. A second procedure appears to be preferable because of obscurity in the field from bleeding of duodenal blood vessels. In this method make a V-shaped slit in the common bile duct before it enters the duodenum and insert a catheter (polyethylene tubing I.D. 0.76 mm = 0.030 inches) into the isolated common bile duct. The catheter length should not exceed 6 inches. Direct the catheter toward the liver. Put two ligatures around the bile duct and tie them to anchor the catheter. If bile flows, determine its rate of flow. The catheter can be filled with heparin–saline solution (1 ml in 99 ml of 0.9% sodium chloride solution) to stimulate flow.

Tie off the ligatures around the vagus nerve and cut between them. Stimulate the caudal end of the vagus nerve with repeated shocks from an electronic stimulator and note the effect on the rate and volume of biliary secretion.

Inject 15 ml of 0.4% hydrochloric acid solution into the duodenum above the bile duct opening and observe whether the presence of acid influences biliary flow.

Inject into the duodenum a solution of sodium dehydrocholate. You can use 2 ml of warmed Decholin sodium (Dome Laboratories, Division of Miles Laboratories, West Haven, Connecticut). A 5-ml ampul is a convenient size, each ampul containing a 20% aqueous solution. Each milliliter is 0.2 gm. Observe the increased flow of a watery bile and explain the mechanism of the increase.

Exercise 11   Normal Hematologic Values in the Rabbit

Three highly related items are to be determined, namely, the red cell count, the hemoglobin concentration, and the packed red cell volume. From the data obtained, several so-called "absolute corpuscular values" can be computed for rabbit blood. Use adult rabbits.

For the red cell count and hemoglobin concentration, collect free-flowing blood from an incision made in an ear vein. The blood pipettes should be clean and dry, and the special diluting fluids should be immediately available.

For the packed cell volume study, the blood can be collected with a syringe and needle wetted with a minimum of heparin, or else the blood may be allowed to drop from a punctured vein into a tube containing any isotonic anticoagulant. One very common anticoagulant is prepared as follows: potassium oxalate, 0.8 gm; ammonium oxalate, 1.2 gm; water to 100.0 ml.

Add 0.1 ml of this anticoagulant solution to a chemically clean Pyrex test tube and evaporate the water to dryness in an oven at 60°–70°C. Do not heat the tube too long, or over 70°C, or the oxalate may be converted into carbonate. Use paraffined corks or rubber stoppers. Each 0.1 ml of this anticoagulant suffices to anticoagulate 1 ml of drawn blood.

TECHNICAL DIRECTIONS

1. Total Erythrocyte Count

Using a calibrated red cell Thoma pipette, draw the blood to the 0.5 mark and fill with Hayem's fluid to the 101 mark. The blood is diluted 1 to 200. Even though the pipette is marked 101, the last figure 1 corresponds to the capillary stem where no dilution occurs. The preparation of Hayem's fluid is as follows: sodium chloride, 1 gm; mercuric chloride, 0.5 gm; sodium sulfate, 5 gm; distilled water to 200 ml.

The hemacytometer counting chamber with double Neubauer ruling and its special cover slip should be cleaned cautiously but thoroughly with water, and dried with lens paper. When filling the pipette, do not allow air bubbles to be sucked in, and fill the pipette exactly to each mark. Close both ends of the pipette and shake it in spiral fashion for 5 minutes. Before filling the counting chamber, blow out the first few drops from the pipette.

Touch a drop of fluid to the surface of the ruled area of the chamber, allowing it to run under the cover glass. The suspension should not flow into the moats on either side nor should any bubbles occur under the cover glass. Allow 3 or more minutes for the cells to spread evenly.

Examine the cells under high power, counting in the central ruled area. This contains 25 blocks of 16 squares each, or a total of 400 small squares. For random sampling, the count is to be made in 5 blocks. Use 4 corners and one center block. Count the cells lying on the lines bounding the squares above and to the left, but not below and to the right. Wide variations in count among the blocks indicate improper dilution of the sample or improper filling of the chamber or not allowing sufficient time for the cells to spread.

Calculate the red cell count. Multiply the observed count by 5 to obtain the number of cells in 25 blocks, or 1 mm². Multiply by 10 to obtain the count in 1 mm³. Then multiply by 200, since the blood was originally diluted to contain 1/200 part of the cells.

To clean the pipette, expel the contents, fill it with water to wash out the cell suspension, draw in 95% alcohol, and then draw in ether followed by air. Avoid alcohol and ether in cleaning the hemacytometer chamber.

Many laboratories now use electronic counters to determine blood cell counts. There are two systems of automated counting. In the Coulter counter a change in electrical conductivity occurs when a red cell passes through an aperture and displaces some of the electrolyte fluid in which it is suspended.

The sequential multiple analysis models are electrooptical. They function by true counting with an automated system.

The Coulter counter should be demonstrated if available.

2. Hemoglobin Concentration

The directions are for the Sahli hemometer, which provides for student laboratories a sufficient accuracy of result (about 5%). Draw up blood in the special Sahli pipette to the 20 mm³ mark, wipe the tip, and immediately expel the blood into the special Sahli tube, in which there has been previously placed 0.1 N HCl exactly to the 10 mark. The blood should be expelled with the pipette tip beneath the acid level. Rinse this acidified blood up and down in the pipette. Be careful to expel every trace of blood into the tube, and do not permit blood on the outer surface of the pipette to be discarded.

Let the tube stand exactly 10 minutes, and then only, begin diluting with distilled water, drop by drop, stirring with a glass rod after each addition, until the depth of brown color (hematin) exactly matches that of the permanent standard in the comparison colorimeter.

The hemoglobin may be read from the tube in gm/100 ml of blood, or less preferably in percentage. The reading is the level of the diluted acidified blood. Note that the percentage values vary with different tubes. Perhaps the most acceptable values are based historically upon Van Slyke determinations with oxygen capacity at 21 volume %, in which 100 % hemoglobin equals 15.6 gm.

There are several different instruments to determine hemoglobin concentration. The more accurate ones include spectrophotometers and other electronic instruments, e.g., the Coulter counter.

3. The Packed Cell Volume

Use the Wintrobe hematocrit tube. By means of a pipette with a capillary tip draw whole blood, anticoagulated with heparin or with a dried mixture of ammonium and potassium oxalate, into the graduated Wintrobe tube. Fill the tube from the bottom up, avoiding air bubbles or breaks in the column of blood. The optimal time between drawing the blood and the beginning of centrifugation is 10 minutes. Centrifuge the blood at not less than 3000 rpm for at least 30 minutes. The blood will have separated into a clear colorless column of plasma and a solid column of cells. The uppermost layer of the solid column is whitish. Read from the graduations on the tube the meniscus of the underlying solid red column, and also the meniscus of the liquid column. Compute the percentage of red cells (PCV) in the total column length.

The chief sources of error in the PCV include: (1) centrifuging at low speeds and for insufficient time; (2) the use of anticoagulants that are not isotonic; and (3) allowing the blood to stand in the Wintrobe tube for too long a time before centrifugation.

The normal values for the rabbit with sex differences considered (Wintrobe et al., 1936) are listed as: red cell count, $6.25–6.30 \times 10^6/\text{c.mm}^3$; hemoglobin, 12.9–13.4 gm/100 ml; packed cell volume, 39.4–40.1 %.

Calculate the following values:

1. Mean corpuscular volume (MCV) in cubic microns

$$\frac{\text{Volume of red cells (in ml) in 1000 ml of blood (hematocrit)}}{\text{Red cells per mm}^3 \text{ (in millions)}}$$

2. Mean corpuscular hemoglobin (MCHb) in micromicrograms

$$\frac{\text{Hemoglobin (in gm) in 1000 ml of blood}}{\text{Red cells per mm}^3 \text{ (in millions)}}$$

3. Mean corpuscular hemoglobin concentration percent (MCHbC) in grams

$$\frac{\text{Hemoglobin (in gm) in 100 ml of blood}}{\text{Volume of red cells in 100 ml of blood}} \text{ (hematocrit)} \times 100$$

Exercise 12 White Blood Cells

The exercise is designed primarily to give experience in counting and differentiating white blood cells, and secondarily to illustrate the influence of psychic factors upon the count. This exercise can be divided into two parts, the part involving smears being done as a single experiment.

Obtain peripheral blood by needle puncture of an ear vein. The vessels should be slightly dilated before puncture by warmth from an electric light bulb. The rabbit previously should have been deprived of food for 16 to 24 hours, to minimize the influence of digestion and absorption.

To obtain the blood in the "normal" and "recovery" periods, the rabbit is to be in a quiet resting position. To produce undue excitement and observe its effects, restrain the animal for about 10 minutes by keeping it on its back, in which position it is stimulated by weak interrupted current from a stimulator for 2 or 3 minutes.

Collect the blood samples in a clean, dry, white cell pipette, drawing the blood exactly to the 0.5 mark, and quickly wiping off excess blood from the tip. Immediately draw in diluting fluid to the 11 mark above the bulb, and then essentially follow the technique described for the red cell count. Count the four corner groups of 16 squares under a low power, and take an average. Multiply the result by 20 (dilution) and then by 10 (depth). Use as a diluent 3% acetic acid just tinged with Gentian Violet.

To observe the types of white cells and make a differential count, use stained smears. Touch a clean slide to a drop of blood from the ear vein, and apply the edge of a second slide over the drop. When the blood has spread underneath the width of the edge of the second slide, glide it smoothly toward the clean end of the under slide, pulling the blood behind it. This leaves a thin film of blood, which must be thoroughly dried. The slides should be stained on the day they are made.

Cover the dried smear with Wright's stain for 2 or 3 minutes. The actual contact time must be determined by trial and error. Do not let the stain evaporate. Flood the slide with distilled water, or preferably with Wright's stain buffer solution (pH 6.4), but do not allow the fluid to run over the edges. Let the mixture stand 3 to 5 minutes. Wash off the stain under running tap water. Wipe away the film of stain from the back of the slide, and let the slide dry in air, standing it on end.

Observe the leukocytes, differentiating them with the aid of commonly available textbook illustrations. Compare the granulocytic series with the lymphocytes and monocytes. Determine the percentage of each major kind of white cell in a large field containing 100 leukocytes.

Designated members of the student team should collect blood (1) in the normal quiet animal, (2) during excitement, and (3) in the recovery period. These samples are to be counted in the hemacytometer chamber, and the data examined for any marked psychic effects. Nice and Katz (1936) found a marked leucopenia in peripheral blood during excitement.

Normal "resting" values for rabbit blood, taken from Kracke (1947) are listed below.

Cells counted	Average	Range
Total white count	7900/mm^3	4000–13,000/mm^3
Differential count		
Neutrophiles	43.4%	30–50%
Lymphocytes	41.8%	30–50%
Monocytes	9.0%	2–16%
Eosinophiles	2.0%	0.5–5%
Basophiles	4.3%	2–6%

We have found depression in the total count ranging from 15 to 30% of the normal while the animals were excited. The white count returns gradually to the quiet, resting level.

Exercise 13   The Platelet Count and the Clotting Time of the Blood; Effects of Parathyroid Hormone

Injection of parathyroid hormone into rabbits many years ago was found to decrease the clotting time and increase the platelet count (Blume and Fang, 1937). The reasons are obscure and do not seem to be directly related to changes in serum calcium. The purpose of repeating this historic work is to provide experience in basic hematologic procedures, such as blood platelet counting and determining the clotting time by a simple capillary procedure.

Each group of students is to obtain a sample of ear blood from a rabbit, upon which the clotting time and platelet count are to be immediately determined according to the methods below. The platelets can also be qualitatively estimated by preparing blood smears treated with Wright's stain.

Obtain parathyroid extract solution. A convenient size is a 5-ml ampul (Lilly) which contains 100 U.S.P. units/ml. Inject 0.25 ml of the solution intravenously. After 10 minutes withdraw a second blood sample from an ear vein. Repeat these samplings at three more successive 15-minute intervals, and determine immediately the clotting time and platelet count for every sample. Record the times of blood withdrawal.

Plot the clotting time in minutes on the ordinate against the time on the abscissa at which the samples were drawn. Similarly plot the number of platelets/mm³ against the blood withdrawal times.

Blume and Fang found the clotting time to be decreased by 40 to 70%, and the platelet count to be increased from 25 to 40%. Compare your results.

TECHNICAL DIRECTIONS

1. Blood Platelet Count

The diluting fluid is 3.8% sodium citrate tinged with Gentian Violet. This is stored in the cold and filtered before use. All glassware must be scrupulously clean.

Draw blood cautiously into the red cell pipette exactly to the 0.5 mark and fill immediately with the diluting fluid exactly to the 101 mark. A 1:200 dilution is obtained. Shake the pipette in spiral fashion for 5 minutes, holding both ends closed; then blow out several drops from the stem, and fill the double Neubauer blood cell counting chamber. The suspension should not flow into the moats on either side, nor should there be bubbles under the cover glass.

Let the solution settle for 15 minutes. Keep the chamber from drying by placing it under a bowl with moist filter paper.

Count the platelets under high power in the large center square which has an area of 1 mm². This is ruled into 25 little blocks, each with 16 small squares, making a total of 400 small squares. Count the cells in 5 blocks (80 small squares). Use 4 corners and one central block. Count the cells lying on the lines bounding the squares above and to the left, but not below and to the right.

If the count is not done immediately, seal the pipette and place it horizontally in the refrigerator. Discard the blood if the cells are hemolyzed. Count only highly refractile forms, and avoid counting debris.

The platelet count should not show wide variations among the 5 blocks examined. Variations indicate improper dilution or improper filling of the chamber or else not allowing sufficient time for the cells to settle.

To compute the count, multiply the number found in 5 blocks of 80 squares by 5, which represents the number in the total 400 squares, or 1 mm². Then multiply this by 10 to obtain the count in 1 mm³. Finally, multiply by 200, since the blood was originally diluted to contain 1/200 part of the cells.

The average platelet count in the untreated normal adult rabbit is 400,000/mm³, with a range of 200,000–1,000,000 (Kracke, 1947).

To clean the pipette, fill it with water or an anticoagulant to expel the cell suspension; draw in 95% ethyl alcohol; then fill the pipette with ether followed by a stream of air. In cleaning the counting chamber, avoid alcohol and ether and use only distilled water, drying the chamber by gentle application of soft lens paper.

All blood cell counts can be expedited in laboratories having electronic blood cell counters (e.g., Coulter).

2. Blood Clotting Time

Draw out small-bore glass tubing to capillary diameter. Make several capillary tubes about 3 inches long.

Draw the blood without using anticoagulants, noting the exact time of its withdrawal, and fill a small tube by capillary action. Hold the tube between the thumb and index finger of both hands, and gently break the tube every 30 seconds until a strand of fibrin appears.

The interval between the withdrawal of blood and the first definite sign of a fibrin strand is the clotting time.

The clotting time at 25°C is reported as 4–5 minutes (Weisbroth *et al.*, 1974). We find that the blood may clot in less time. Such variations are linked partly with differences in the breeds of rabbits and with the condition of the glass tubes and the sizes of the tubes.

Exercise 14   Prothrombin Time (Quick's Method)

If excess thromboplastin and calcium are added to plasma, *in vitro*, prothrombin conversion to thrombin is promoted, and the time for clot formation is a direct index of prothrombin concentration.

The thromboplastin used may be prepared by the student, following the directions below, or it may be obtained commercially. Use fresh thromboplastin, otherwise the prothrombin time becomes prolonged. We have obtained variations from a 25-second to a 65-second time with aging thromboplastin. Also, commercial thromboplastin should be pure and not contain calcium.

A. PREPARATION OF THROMBOPLASTIN

Kill a rabbit by injecting 20 ml of air into an ear vein; remove the calvarium (top of the skull) and bring out the brain, clearing it of all blood vessels.

Add 0.1 ml of 0.2 M sodium citrate solution to the brain in a mortar, and cover the organ with acetone. Mash the brain within a 10-minute period to a granular powder, renewing the acetone several times. Dry the material by suction in a Buchner funnel, and then by incubation at 37°C for 15 minutes.

Weigh the desiccated brain and add 0.85% sodium chloride solution, in the ratio of 5 ml to each 0.2 gm of dried material. Mix the solution thoroughly and incubate it at once for 20 minutes in a water bath not ex ceeding 49–50°C.

The supernatant fluid and coarse particles are not to be separated, but the suspension should be mixed before use. The thromboplastin so prepared should give a "normal" prothrombin time (11–15 seconds in human blood) and should not be used if the time becomes prolonged. It will remain stable for perhaps 18 hours if refrigerated.

B. DETERMINATION OF PROTHROMBIN TIME

Cut down on the internal jugular vein of a rabbit anesthetized with sodium pentobarbital, and quickly draw 4.5 ml of blood into a previously cooled syringe, using a 20-gauge needle. The vein should be entered cleanly without getting any tissue fluid into the needle. It is not difficult with practice in unanesthetized rabbits to utilize an ear vein or to employ direct cardiac puncture, but clotting and insufficient volumes are hard to avoid in marginal vein sampling, and a mixture with tissue juices is a hazard in intracardiac punctures.

Place the blood at once in a centrifuge tube containing 0.5 ml of previously cooled 0.1 M sodium oxalate solution and mix the liquids thoroughly. Centrifuge this sample immediately at 3000 rpm for 15 minutes, and transfer the plasma to a test tube.

To a 0.1-ml sample of plasma in a small test tube (13 mm outside diameter), add 0.1 ml of thromboplastin, mixing all contents well and keeping the mixture for 1 minute in a water bath. Blow 0.1 ml of 0.025 M

calcium chloride solution (previously warmed to 37°C) into the treated plasma, keeping the liquid in the water bath. Make sure that solutions are put into the blood, using a "blow-out" pipette.

Note the time with a stopwatch from the moment of calcium chloride addition, and repeatedly tilt the tube gently to within a few seconds of the expected clotting time. Under a good light observe the first sign of a fibrin weblike clot, and immediately read the stopwatch.

The time for the fibrin web to form is the prothrombin time. There should be at least two determinations from the 0.1-ml samples of plasma.

Exercise 15 Alterations of Blood Cells by Anticoagulants

The ideal anticoagulant must not only keep blood from clotting, but for studies such as sedimentation rate and cell volume it must not change the overall size of the red cells. This exercise illustrates selection of anticoagulants to these ends, and is adapted from original investigation in the senior author's laboratory.

Each group will work on a separate anticoagulant. Select among the ones in common use, such as sodium citrate, sodium oxalate, potassium oxalate, ammonium potassium oxalate, lithium oxalate, and sodium fluoride. Obtain 10 ml of blood from the rabbit by direct cardiac puncture, using a No. 18-gauge needle having a 1½-inch stem length. Before use, wet the needle and the dead space of the syringe with a minimum amount of 1% heparin.

Heparin is said not to change the red cell size, so that the heparinized packed red cell volume, which is to be obtained experimentally, may be considered as a standard with which the packed red cell volumes obtained with the test anticoagulants may be compared.

Fill two Wintrobe hematocrit tubes approximately to the 10-mm mark with the heparinized blood. These tubes should be centrifuged after standing 10 minutes, and the two packed cell volumes averaged.

To each of a series of Wintrobe tubes, add a single anticoagulant solution to the 1-mm mark. Vary the concentration of each anticoagulant so that a series of dilution is obtained, ranging from hypertonic solutions in some tubes to hypotonic solutions in others. Identify each tube with markings.

Add heparinized blood to each tube up to the 10-mm graduation, put on the rubber stoppers that fit the Wintrobe tubes, and let them stand 10 minutes. Then centrifuge the tubes, along with the two standards, at 3000 rpm for 30 minutes. Read the height of the packed red cells as well as the total height of the combined cell and liquid column. The packed cell volume in percent is computed from the ratio of red cells to total column (minus the height due to white cells and anticoagulant) x 100. No correction need be made in any tube for the small volume of heparin mixed with the plasma.

Draw a graph of packed cell volume against concentration, making a horizontal line for the packed cell volume of the heparin standard. The intercept of the test curve with the heparin line represents the concentration of the anticoagulant that is not only isosmolar with blood but also isotonic (causes no swelling or shrinkage of the cells). If the curve does not appear to behave as though an ideal semipermeable system existed, explain this primarily but not exclusively in terms of ion transport between the red cells and the anticoagulant. This suggests that the most probable isotonic value should be accepted only from the mean of a statistical series of values.

Observe that the anticoagulants were mixed in the ratio of 1 volume to 9 volumes of blood. One student team might work with the isotonic concentrations of each anticoagulant, to discover whether these proportions are truly correct for proper anticoagulation, and to find the optimal proportions.

Perhaps the greatest variable in this exercise is the length of time the blood stands in the Wintrobe tube before it is centrifuged.

It should be emphasized that although ideally osmotic anticoagulants can be established for hematologic purposes, they may not be entirely suitable for blood-chemistry studies. Whereas the mixture of ammonium and potassium oxalate is the anticoagulant of choice for the preservation of blood cells, it produces abnormally high values of urea nitrogen and nonprotein nitrogen. Heparin or potassium fluoride would be more suitable for the analysis of chemical constituents. Heparin, itself, should not be used to determine the sedimentation rate.

From a theoretical standpoint, the concentration of the test solution that is isomotic with blood may be computed from freezing-point data of rabbit blood, and from G values of those anticoagulants that are listed in the literature, or else assumed to be the same as the values established for human blood. Attention should be given in this regard to freezing-point depression data and G values listed in the International Critical Tables and elsewhere.

As examples of the experimental ranges of values to be expected, 0.69–0.70% of sodium fluoride, 3.82–3.88% of sodium citrate, and 1.3% of sodium oxalate were found in our laboratory to be isotonic with rabbit blood.

Isomotic solutions can be approximated, knowing the valence and molecular weight of the solute, the freezing-point (ΔT) of the blood of any species with which the solute is being compared, and assuming total dissociation of the solute. Thus, for turtle blood, with which the senior author has done work, and using sodium oxalate where three ions form: Suppose (1) ΔT for turtle blood is found to be $- 0.522°C$. (2) ΔT for a one molal solution of any ideal nonelectrolyte is $-1.86°C$. (3) Molecular weight of sodium oxalate is 134.01. Then $(0.522/1.86) \times (134.01/3) =$ 12.54 gm/liter = solution of sodium oxalate which is isomotic with turtle blood.

The ratio of the two ΔT's above is called the G value, or the isotonic coefficient. The ratio indicates that a given concentration of an electrolyte has a ΔT a certain number of times greater than that of a nonelectrolyte.

To illustrate an associated usage of the above ratio 0.522/1.86, or 0.28, if ΔT of 0.25 M lithium oxalate is experimentally determined to be 1.192, then $1.192/(1.86 \times 0.25)$ equals 2.56, or G_2. The ratio G_1/G_2, or 0.28/2.56, gives a molarity, 0.109, of the solution that has a ΔT equal to $-0.522°$. A lithium oxalate solution of this molarity is isomolar with turtle blood.

We emphasize that the isomotic value is that obtained by theoretical computation. This must be adjusted to the isotonic value which is the figure to be used in actual practice. An isotonic solution does not change the size of the cell immersed in that solution.

Exercise 16   Total Blood and Plasma Volume

A. THEORY

Fluids are distributed in plasma, tissue spaces, lymph, and cells. The knowledge of the measurement of the fluid volume in the blood plasma, especially, is essential to a solution of the problems of fluid imbalance that can arise in the rabbit following surgery.

One estimate of the total blood volume of an adult rabbit is that it is about 6% of the body weight, or 136 ml in the 5-lb (2268-gm) animal. The plasma volume is at least 50% of the 136, or 68 ml.

Numerical values stated for vital data on the rabbit and also on many other laboratory animals are extremely variable and much standardization is yet to occur. An early paper of Downman et al. (1944) reports the blood volume of the rabbit to be 70 ml/kg of body weight. These investigators also state that rabbits which are not anesthetized, or else only lightly anesthetized with urethane, can lose up to one-third of their total blood volume without signs of distress and without any grossly observable deterioration in their health and activity.

Courtice and Gunton (1949) cite the plasma volume of the adult rabbit to be 39.8 ml/kg and the total blood volume to be 57.7 ml/kg. Their data are based on photoelectric methods.

The plasma volume is to be determined in this exercise by a dilution principle. One must know (1) the quantity in milliliters of the nontoxic dye injected into the plasma (in which fluid it must be restricted and in which it must not fade), and (2) the concentration of the dye per milliliter of plasma after thorough dispersion in the plasma.

$$\text{Plasma volume (ml)} = \frac{\text{milliliters of dye injected}}{\text{concentration of dye per milliliter of plasma}}$$

B. PROCEDURE

Use vital dye T-1824 (Evans blue). For a 5 mg/ml solution find the wavelength on a spectrophotometer which gives the greatest percentage transmission. Use this wavelength for the procedure to follow. Make known dilutions of this dye concentration and take readings on the spectrophotometer. Plot a graph of percentage transmission versus concentration. Thus, unknown concentrations can be determined by interpolation.

To obtain a control blank, collect a blood sample in a centrifuge tube which has been rinsed with heparin. Centrifuge this sample. Read the percentage transmission in the spectrophotometer. This reading should be subtracted from all the unknown (test) readings.

For any blood sample collected, or for injections, either (1) anesthetize the rabbit and cut down on the femoral or jugular vein, or the carotid artery, or (2) inject into ear veins and collect by cardiac puncture.

Using an ear vein, inject with syringe and 25-gauge needle 2 ml of the dye (in a concentration of 5 mg/ml). The dye does get partly lost from the circulation so the rate of loss must be considered. Therefore, obtain three samples of blood—in this case by cardiac puncture at 10, 20, and 30 minutes after dye injection; each blood sample is 5 ml. For each sample, obtain plasma by centrifugation (3000 rpm for up to ½ hour).

The plasma sample obtained is colored. Determine the concentration of dye in each sample, by using the spectrophotometer and calibrated graph.

Plot the plasma volumes on the ordinate of semilog paper against time in minutes on the abscissa. To get the true plasma volume, extrapolate back to zero time and read the ordinate value (volume at time of injection).

Since the dye does not enter red blood cells, the procedure does not measure total blood volume. Obtain the hematocrit value of a sample of whole blood and use the equation:

$$\text{Blood volume} = \text{true plasma volume} \times \frac{100}{100 - 0.87 \text{ hematocrit}}$$

Exercise 17   Splenectomy

The spleen is large and accessible in the rabbit. This surgical exercise thus readily follows the one on laparotomy to develop manipulative skill.

The functions of the spleen are illustrated by the effect following its surgical removal. Many of its activities are not definitely known. It is said to maintain a reserve supply of red cells. By virtue of contractility, it delivers the red cells to the peripheral blood stream. It can make red cells more susceptible to hemolysis. It may prepare "B" lymphocytes to manufacture antibodies. In the fetus it actively produces red cells and forms bilirubin from the breakdown of hemoglobin.

PROCEDURE

Anesthetize a rabbit with sodium pentobarbital, and follow with an inhalant anesthetic if necessary. The rabbit should have been fasted to minimize bowel size and to facilitate adequate exposure of the splenic region.

Make an incision along the linea alba, extending from the caudal border of the rib cage to the mid-abdominal level. Expose the spleen in the upper-left quadrant of the abdominal cavity. Observe that it is held, not by a single pedicle, but is fixed by its mesentery and by four or more blood vessels. Isolate the major splenic artery and inject 0.5 ml of 1:1000 epinephrine solution to produce a sudden dramatic shrinking of the organ.

Ligate each blood vessel separately. Use a medium-to-small, curved, surgical needle, and extrafine (size 00) chromic catgut. Clamp the needle within the jaws of a needle holder in undertaking the suturing.

Remove any splenic adhesions by blunt dissection with the fingers. Place two clamps on the splenic "pedicle," at least 2 cm apart and both on the splenic side of the ligature that has already been made.

Divide the pedicle by cutting between the two clamps (hemostats or bulldog clamps). Release the clamp nearer to the ligature and observe whether there is any bleeding from the stump. If the field is dry, remove the clamps. When all ligated blood vessels have been divided and there is no evidence of bleeding, deliver the spleen through the operative field.

Close the peritoneum and abdominal muscles at one time with a continuous suture. Use catgut for the internal sutures. Bring the edges of the skin together with Vetafil, using interrupted or mattress sutures.

Let the rabbit recover in a warm room which is properly supervised. Provide drinking water, but withhold food the first postoperative day. After one or more weeks, do several functional tests; these should also have been done on the animal prior to operation, to show what is changed or lost after splenectomy.

Several tests are feasible. It is suggested that these include (1) hemoglobin determination, to reveal progressive anemia; (2) blood smears, to show any change in lymphocyte formation; (3) packed cell volume to show any effects upon the percentage of red cell; and (4) clotting time, which seems to increase sharply after splenectomy.

Other tests may be done. Check an increased resistance to hemolysis or decreased fragility of the red cells by an osmotic fragility test. The platelets may increase, as seen in a cell count performed electronically or with a hemacytometer.

Make a record of the body weight, rectal temperature, and general physical condition of the rabbit before and for one or more weeks after surgery.

Exercise 18   **Perfusion of the Isolated Heart**

Excise the whole heart and vessels of a freshly killed rabbit, wash these organs free of blood, and tie a cannula into the aorta. Suspend the heart from the cannula, which is fixed to a support and connected by tubing to a reservoir such as an aspirator bottle. Raise the bottle to a height sufficient to drive the fluid into the heart under pressure. Fill the reservoir with Ringer's solution to which glucose is added and arrange to keep the fluid at 37° C, with a continuous supply of oxygen bubbling rapidly through it. Control the flow by a clamp on the tubing so that the fluid drops slowly through the cardiac cannula. Enclose the heart in a warmed chamber or let warm, oxygenated Ringer's solution drip over it.

Direct the cannula toward the aortic valves, which are brought into apposition by the perfusion pressure. The fluid then passes through the coronary arteries and leaves through the right atrium. Record the atrial and ventricular contractions in the classic method by two heart levers writing on a kymograph drum, or preferably by transduction, amplification, and channel recording (Fig. 21).

Investigate the influence of ions on the heart. Connect a second bottle by a T-tube to the flow from the first bottle. Regulate the two flows by Hoffman clamps so that the composition of the perfusion fluid at the level of the heart can be modified at will. Observe the effects of altering the concentrations of cations. Try changing the concentrations of sodium chloride, potassium chloride, and calcium chloride in the Ringer's solution. Have every solution available and warmed.

Test the influence of pH by using weak acids or alkalis.

Drugs can be added to the Ringer's solution. The most convenient way to introduce the drug is to inject it with a hypodermic syringe into the final outlet tubing from the aspirator bottles. Observe the effects of epinephrine, acetylcholine, and any other drug desired, upon the rate, force, and regularity of the heart.

Insert a glass tube through the superior vena cava into the right atrium. Pass Ringer's solution at several controlled temperatures through the tube, and note the effects of warming and of cooling the sinoatrial node.

Observe the effects of asphyxiation upon the properties of the heartbeat by cutting off the oxygen supply from the perfusion fluid.

Obtain the records by manual or by electronic apparatus. In using the

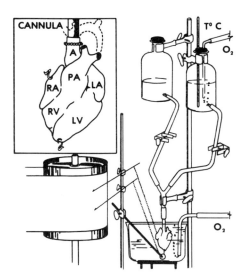

Figure 21. Perfusion apparatus. Diagram of laboratory perfusion apparatus for isolated heart.

electronic equipment pierce the heart at its apex with a hook. Connect the hook by a fine thread to a transducer. In turn, connect the transducer to an amplification system and the latter in turn to a channel recorder. The recorder can be a pen-writer since the frequency of the heartbeat is sufficiently slow. A separate event and time marker record both the start of events and the duration of time involved in the occurrence of the events.

In our use of a Physiograph system (Narco Bio-Systems, Houston, Texas) for student work, we obtain the signals with a compatible myograph instrument. This is a photoelectric force transducer which quantitatively measures cardiac muscle contractions. The output of the myograph goes to the channel amplifier. The amplifier provides the required increase in signal strength while maintaining a proportional relationship between the electrical signal and the physiologic activity which it represents (see Fig. 22 and 23). Any other electronic system can be substituted.

Exercise 19 Hemodynamics

A. RETINAL BLOOD FLOW

Examine the eyes of an untreated, unanesthetized rabbit with an ophthalmoscope. Observe the movements in the retinal blood vessels. Do you see individual erythrocytes? Note the rate and general appearance of the cellular flow.

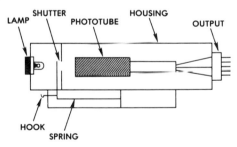

Figure 22.   Myograph. Longitudinal section of myograph.

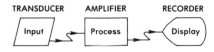

Figure 23.   Electronic recording. Information flow in electronic recording.

B. ARTERIAL BLOOD PRESSURE

An indirect method was historically introduced (McGregor, 1928) in an intact unanesthetized rabbit. Gently place the animal down in prone position on the surgical table. To minimize excitation, let the rabbit lie quietly for at least 5 minutes.

Place an inflatable cuff, about 12 cm wide, around the abdomen, so that its lower border makes a snug fit just above the iliac crest. Slip under the inferior border the flat chest piece (about 3 cm in diameter) of a stethoscope. If placed in a midline position, it lies over the termination and bifurcation of the abdominal aorta. The chest piece may be fixed to the table by lateral tapes. Connect the cuff to a clinical sphygmomanometer. Do not position the cuff too far caudally.

Inflate the cuff to about 200 torr, which obliterates the aorta, gradually release the pressure, and obtain the first or systolic sound. Take the diastolic reading where there is a distinct muffling of the sounds which should be just above the last audible sound. The method of palpation may also be tried to obtain the systolic pressure. When the cuff is first being slowly released, palpate the femoral artery in the groin for the first pulse wave. This is difficult to obtain in so small an animal. In the method of auscultation the first reading is discarded, and the next three are averaged. If struggling occurs, repeat the trials after 5 to 10 minutes. In the original paper, McGregor reported a blood pressure in torr of 125/90 as an average of 1120 readings on 84 rabbits.

If desired, inject intravenously 1 ml of 1:1000 epinephrine solution, and obtain serial blood pressure readings for at least ½ hour.

Cite your opinion about whether constriction of the abdomen in this method is unphysiologic. What agreement do you obtain in the method of palpation? What is the effect of repeated determinations on the blood pressure? Is "averaging" a valid procedure?

C. STEPHEN HALES' EXPERIMENT

In 1733 Hales inserted a vertical tube into the crural (femoral) artery of a mare, and the blood rose to a height of 8 feet, 3 inches (or 254 cm) above the left ventricle, with a variation of about 2 inches (about 5 cm) with each heartbeat.

Use an adult rabbit as in the above experiment. Inject 1 ml of heparin into an ear vein. Anesthetize the animal, do a cut down on the carotid artery, and ligate the vessel with two bulldog clamps about 1 inch apart. Cut a V-shaped notch in the artery between the clamps and insert a cannula, binding it down with a ligature. Attach a glass tube about 0.1 inches (0.25 cm) in diameter and about 7 feet (213 cm) in length by a rubber connection to the cannula, fixing it in vertical position. In addition to the heparin injection, wet the cannula and the glass tube with 3.8% sodium citrate solution. Release the proximal bulldog clamp, allowing the blood from the heart to ascend its full height in the vertical tube. Record the height attained from the level of the left ventricle. What does this represent in terms of millimeters of mercury (torr) blood pressure? Can you detect small variations in pressure due to systole and diastole of the heart? With the blood pressure of the horse in mind, is there much variation of blood pressure with the size of an animal?

A rise of about 60 inches (152 cm) can be expected. The loss of blood influences the pressure and the height attained. Saline can be injected through the femoral vein to restore pressure.

In converting, for example, a 55-inch rise of the blood to millimeters of mercury:

$$\frac{1}{25.4 \text{ mm}} = \frac{55}{x}$$

where x = 1397 mm of blood. Considering the density of mercury:

$$\frac{1397}{13.6} = 102 \text{ mm of mercury}$$

Exercise 20 **Circulation Time**

A. USE OF METHYLENE BLUE

Inject 5% sodium pentobarbital solution very slowly into an ear vein. Follow with an inhalant anesthetic if necessary.

Expose the carotid artery and place under it a strip of white glazed paper. Focus a strong light onto the artery. Into the jugular vein of the opposite side introduce a cannula pointed toward the heart. To the cannula attach a burette filled with a saturated solution of methylene blue in isotonic sodium choride solution. Have the solution at 37° C.

Fill the cannula and the connections with this fluid. Hold the burette upright with the fluid at a high level. Remove a preset clamp from the vein and, at a signal from an observer with a stopwatch, open the burette and allow 1 ml of the contents to enter the vein very rapidly. The observer immediately notes the time when the blue appears in the carotid artery.

Since the methylene blue is quickly reduced to a colorless compound, repeat this observation. Inject the same amount of colored fluid each time, and record the average of the observations. The time thus determined is considered to be the pulmonary circulation time.

We have found that injection of 1 ml of India ink often produces more visible results than methylene blue does and that India ink is tolerated by the rabbit in the dose employed.

B. USE OF ACETYLCHOLINE

A method originally proposed for the dog by Wilburne *et al.*, (1947) has been adapted here for the rabbit. In a fasted rabbit anesthetized with sodium pentobarbital, open the chest by a midline incision. Avoid any manipulation that would tear the diaphragm or produce a fatal pneumothorax. Using a 20-gauge needle attached to a tuberculin syringe, inject rapidly 10 mg (0.2 ml of a 5% solution) of acetylcholine chloride into the aorta, directing the needle away from the heart. A prolonged circulation time will result if the injection period exceeds 1 second and if the solution volume is too large.

The end point is the transitory inhibition of the sinus node or A-V junction. This is determined most simply by auscultation or pulse palpation where the end point is the first prolonged heartbeat. Measure the circulation time with a stopwatch from the start of injection to a point where an expected auricular or ventricular response fails to occur on time.

Record the end point alternatively with an electrocardiograph. Indicate the time of injection on the ECG record by simultaneously deflecting the lead marker.

Take care to allow very little blood to back up into the injecting syringe, since acetylcholine is destroyed quickly by blood cholinesterase. List the circulation time as "superior vena cava time," " root of aorta time," or "2 to 3 cm above the root of the aorta time." Take the average of several trials.

Exercise 21   Arterial Blood Pressure by Cannulation

Every student should learn to obtain blood pressure recordings by direct cannulation of the exposed carotid artery.

Anesthetize a rabbit lightly with sodium pentobarbital, and follow with ether or other inhalation anesthetic as needed.

Directions have been given earlier in the text for cannulating the carotid artery. A cannula should also be inserted into a femoral vein for injections.

The surgeon exposes the structures in the following order: right carotid artery, right and left vagus nerves, and the left femoral vein. He should know in advance every step he is to take.

The surgeon's assistant provides clean instruments, including light and heavy forceps and scissors, a knife with a removable blade (such as Bard-Parker or others), blunt-tipped probes, arterial cannulas, artery clips, ligatures, absorbent cotton, and gauze.

The technician or recorder guides the timing and sequence of the instrumental analyzers. He obtains full records of all events, using a channel recorder, set at a speed that distinguishes the individual heartbeats. In laboratories that still use mechanical equipment, the technician manipulates the manometer and washout system as illustrated in the accompanying diagram (Fig. 24). He adjusts the recording levers and operates a signal magnet below the writing stylet of the mercury manometer.

All solutions and instruments must be available because all the manipulations should be performed very quickly. Once a result is obtained, proceed at once to the next step.

A. THE CLASSIC MANUAL MANOMETER SYSTEM

Connect the distal end of the carotid cannula by heavy rubber tubing to a mercury manometer, with a T-tube in the circuit for washout purposes. Fill the entire system through one limb of the manometer from a gravity or pressurized bottle with an anticoagulant solution. This should preferably be a solution containing 1 ml of heparin/100 ml of 0.85%

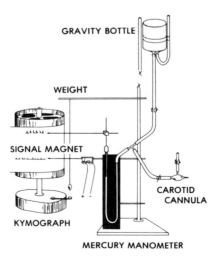

Figure 24. Mercury manometer. Apparatus for recording carotid blood pressure by classic manual method. This system is superseded by transducers and channel recording.

sodium chloride solution. Avoid an anticoagulant such as 25% magnesium sulfate because of its depressive anesthetic effect upon the rabbit.

It is necessary to establish an outside fluid pressure directed toward the artery so that when the clamp of the anticoagulant gravity bottle is released, the solution will be forced into the carotid artery, mix with the blood, and prevent intravascular clotting. In the operated anesthetized rabbit, the blood pressure is about 95–100 torr, making it necessary to establish beforehand an external pressure estimated to balance this. This is done by pumping air into the inlet of the pressure bottle with a rubber bulb whose tubing can be clamped off at the desired pressure. Observe that the blood pressure in torr is twice the distance recorded on the kymograph paper from the zero base line. Use a long paper kymograph or two kymographs carrying a long strip of paper between them. If the respiratory amplitude is great, it is necessary to have the manometer well filled with mercury. When the carotid clamp leading to the mercury manometer is released, the mercury float should oscillate. Operate a signal magnet below the manometer writing point. Remember never to release an artery until the estimated blood pressure is balanced by the mercury column in the manometer. Also, never connect the pressure syringe system with an open artery.

B. ELECTRONIC RECORDING OF BLOOD PRESSURE

A special pressure transducer (e.g., Physiograph Bourdon Photoelectric Transducer) is very useful for converting pressure variations in the carotid artery into electrical signals which are transmitted to an amplifier and in turn to a recording system (usually a pen-/writer, on a channel recorder).

The transducer should have a fluid inlet port. Its outlet end is best fitted with a stopcock for cleaning and flushing. Care must be taken to remove air from the system because the compressibility of air bubbles causes reduction of sensitivity in responses.

A linear transducer, in which voltage conversion to pressure is represented by a straight line, is first calibrated to relate voltage output to the incident pressure. After connecting the transducer to the recording system, the gain of the system can be conveniently set so that 1 cm equals 0.1 V output.

To record carotid artery pressure, place the cannula against the direction of flow. Remember to keep the cannula and tubing entirely filled with fluid and free from air and clots.

C. PROTOCOL BY EITHER METHOD

1. Record the carotid blood pressure. Take a few inches of tracing. Observe the individual pulse beats and the changes of blood pressure with respiration.

2. Place your finger over the cannula opening in the trachea, maintaining the closure until the effects are obvious. Through what stages do the changes pass? What effects upon respiration occur? What are the changes in pulse rate at different stages of asphyxia? Explain how prolonged dyspnea may produce a fall in blood pressure.

3. Obtain another strip of normal tracing; then inject 0.25 ml of epinephrine (1:10,000). Explain the rise in blood pressure. What is the latency of the reaction? What is its complete duration? Is the after-reaction normal or subnormal? How much was the systolic pressure increased? Record the pulse rate during and at the apex of the rise. Is there evidence of cardiac acceleration, and what would cause it?

4. Cut the right vagus between two tightly tied ligatures. Record the effects of stimulating both the central and peripheral ends. After peripheral stimulation what is the effect on the heart rate? Does it appear at once? Is it persistent? Record the pressure at the height of the effective stimulation. Is blood pressure normal or subnormal when the reaction is over?

What is the effect of central stimulation upon respiration, heart rate, and mean blood pressure?

5. Cut the left vagus nerve. Is there any influence upon the respiration not observed when the right nerve alone was sectioned? Stimulate the left nerve centrally and peripherally, and answer under the new conditions all the questions asked in the preceding section.

6. Again inject 0.25 ml of epinephrine and explain the difference in reaction from the first intravenous epinephrine injection.

7. Inject a freshly prepared solution of acetylcholine chloride. Make a 0.1% solution and inject 0.1 ml/kg. This equals 0.10 mg/kg. The toxic dose in the rabbit is about 0.15 mg/kg.

8. If the blood pressure permits, draw off blood from the cannulated vein to observe the effect of hemorrhage. A transfusion of warm saline may then be run in to ascertain the immediate result upon blood pressure.

9. Introduce air by a hypodermic syringe into the vein, and observe the effects upon the blood pressure. After death, open the right atrium and note the bubbles. Explain the effects of air embolism.

10. This is an acute terminal exercise. Make sure that euthanasia is carried out.

Exercise 22   **Factors Influencing Respiration and
Laryngeal Movements**

A. FACTORS INFLUENCING RESPIRATION

Etherize a rabbit and expose the caudal part of the trachea, avoiding
the more cranial pharyngeal and hyoid regions.

Make a double T-shaped incision in the trachea, the long arms pointing in opposite longitudinal directions. Place a cannula pointed toward
the lungs in the lower opening and connect it with the ether bottle as
needed. In the upper opening insert a cannula pointed toward the nasal
cavities.

Expose both vagus nerves in the ventral neck and place loose lifting
ligatures under them. Arrange to record respiration. In laboratories using
manual equipment, rotate a kymograph drum just quickly enough to
resolve individual respiratory cycles. Use either a thread passing from a
pin, placed in the xiphoid skin of the rabbit, to a pulley system and then
to a heart lever, or else use a small animal pneumograph tied around the
rabbit's chest and connected by pressure tubing to a Marey tambour
whose lever writes on the moving drum.

For the newer and more preferable electronic channel recorders (e.g.,
Physiograph system, Narco Bio-Systems, Houston, Texas 77017), impedance pneumographs, and bellows-type pneumographs are available.

The impedance pneumograph is a transducer/preamplifier for the
quantitative measurement of respiratory rates, relative volumes and flow
patterns. Two needles, or two disk or plate electrodes are attached to the
rabbit. A small alternating current is passed through the electrodes. The
voltage across the electrodes is directly proportional to the rabbit's impedance. Voltage changes because of impedance changes are amplified
for pen recording on a channel recorder. The impedance pneumograph
can be connected with the channel recorder.

The alternative bellows-type pneumograph is a photoelectric
transducer that works much like a myograph, but it is specialized to
record thoracic respiratory movements. The Narco Bio-Systems
pneumograph, which can be connected to the Physiograph channel
recorder, consists of a negative pressure transducer with an attached flexible neoprene bellows and an adjustable strap to keep the bellows firmly
adherent to the moving chest wall. Rates, time sequences, and patterns of
movement are visualized on the channel recorder.

Data Collection

Obtain a short record, then lighten the anesthesia as judged by reflexes
and movements, and obtain another strip of respiratory tracings.

Etherize the rabbit deeply through the bottle connected to the lower cannula and observe the effect upon respiration.

Lighten the anesthesia and obtain a record. Then place an ether cone over the nose of the animal and suck ether through the nasal cavities by aspiration through the upper tracheal cannula. Record the effects on the moving paper.

Deeply anesthetize the animal through the lower cannula. Then suck in ether through the nasal cone by aspiration through the upper cannula. Record the effects.

While the rabbit is under deep anesthesia, cut both vagus nerves low in the neck, and allow recovery from the anesthesia. Again aspirate ether through the nasal cone and observe the record.

Summarize the influence of ether upon respiratory reflexes as follows: (a) nasal reflex effects; (b) deep lung reflexes; and (c) the path of the reflexes as shown by the experimental evidence.

B. FACTORS INFLUENCING LARYNGEAL MOVEMENTS

Extend the upper tracheal incision cranially, avoiding the superficial blood vessels which should be tied and reflected with the skin. Expose the thyroid and cricoid cartilages.

Isolate the upper continuation of the vagus nerves and find the superior laryngeal branch on one side. This is given off at the level of origin of the internal carotid artery. It crosses the dorsal side of the common carotid artery to reach the larynx, where it gives sensory fibers to the mucous membrane and motor fibers to the cricothyroid muscle.

Expose the cranial opening of the larynx by cutting transversely across the pharynx between the hyoid bone and the thyroid cartilage. Bring the tip of the epiglottis through the incision and secure it with a hemostat. Enlarge the cut laterally to raise the larynx and examine its internal aspect (Fig. 25).

Data Collection

Identify the glottis and the rudimentary vocal folds. Note the changes in the glottis during quiet respiration, and then make the vocal folds more conspicuous by closing the lower tracheal cannula to produce dyspnea.

Obtain records of all the following procedures. Stimulate the laryngeal mucosa with absorbent cotton and observe inhibition of respiration and forced expiration (coughing).

Stimulate the superior laryngeal nerve with weak faradic current from

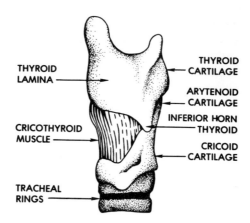

Figure 25.   Larynx. Diagram of larynx in lateral view.

a stimulator and record the effects upon respiration and laryngeal movements.

Cut the superior laryngeal nerve between two ligatures, stimulate its distal and then its central end, and record the effects in each instance.

The laryngeal musculature, except for the cricothyroid, is supplied by the inferior laryngeal nerve. Search for the latter at the inferior aspect of the larynx. Stimulate this nerve with faradic shocks and record its effects upon respiratory movements and upon the action of the laryngeal muscles. Cut the nerve between two ligatures, stimulate its distal and then its central end, and analyze the effects in each instance.

This is an acute terminal exercise. Euthanatize the rabbit with an overdose of the anesthetic used.

Exercise 23   **Neural Aspects of the Regulation of Respiration**

Anesthetize a rabbit with an inhalant drug via a face cone and maintain it throughout the exercise under very light anesthesia. Insert a cannula into the trachea and continue the anesthesia by use of an Erlenmeyer flask equipped with 2-hole stopper. Air is sucked through the anesthetic drug placed in the flask and the mixture is led via the outlet tube into the tracheal cannula.

Expose both vagus nerves and pass loose ligatures around them. Expose one common carotid artery, cannulate it, and fix the cannula in place with two ligatures.

Fully wet the internal barrel of a syringe as well as its needle with 1% heparin, and withdraw 2 ml of blood from the carotid artery. Save the blood sample under mineral oil for a pH determination. Inject warm

0.85% saline solution into the blood vessel.

Record respiration by manual or electronic methods. In the latter method use a bellow-type pneumograph and plug its outlet to the input terminal of a channel recorder. Record time also.

Clamp the trachea at the height of inspiration and note the results. Repeat at the height of expiration. What importance do these observations have?

Ligate one vagus nerve during a recording and cut it distal to the ligature. Repeat this with the opposite vagus. Observe the change in time and length relations of inspiration and expiration and in the amplitude of movements.

Clamp the trachea again in inspiration and in expiration, and contrast the results with those prior to vagotomy.

Stimulate with repeated electric shocks from a stimulator the central end of the right vagus and then of the left vagus nerve, getting subsequent respiratory records. From all observations, what is the apparent role of the vagi in breathing?

Expose the sciatic nerve in the dorsal aspect of the hindlimb and pass a loose ligature around it. While recording respiration, lift the nerve and stimulate it with moderate tetanizing current. Obtain a record.

Clamp the trachea for 2 minutes and obtain a record of respiration. During this clamping, withdraw 2 ml of carotid blood and hold it under oil for a subsequent pH determination; then release the tracheal pressure. Allow several milliliters of blood to escape from the arterial cannula before taking the test sample.

Trephine the skull and transect the brain stem above the medulla. If respiration persists, make lower transections. Estimate at what level the rhythmicity respiratory centers are located.

Perform the pH determinations electrometrically using a glass electrode method (pH meter). Follow the directions accompanying the specific instrument. The pH of rabbit blood is 7.35 with a range of 7.21–7.57.

Exercise 24   Temperature Regulation in Homotherms

Each group may contain two or three students who are responsible for a single phase of the procedure. One group injects a rabbit intraperitoneally with magnesium chloride ($MgCl_2 \cdot 6H_2O$), 3 mg/kg body weight. This makes the animal cold-blooded, but at this dose the drug is neither an anesthetic nor is it curarizing. Before injection, keep this rabbit for one-half hour at an environmental temperature of 20°C, which may be considered a thermoneutral environment for the rabbit. Record the rectal temperature.

After injecting the drug, place the rabbit in a refrigator at 2°–6°C. Let it equilibrate therein for one-half hour. Following this, take rectal temperatures at three 10-minute intervals. Note the lack of defense against the cold environment. The respiration, for example, may increase rather than decrease.

Warm the treated rabbit to room temperature. Let it equilibrate for one-half hour, than take rectal temperatures at three 10-minute intervals.

Next, warm the rabbit in a chamber at about 35°C. (A cage containing portable lamps is satisfactory.) Let equilibration take place for one-half hour and obtain rectal temperature readings at three 10-minute periods thereafter. Observe the responses of the treated rabbit to the elevated room temperature.

A second student group repeats the entire procedure outlined, but does not inject magnesium chloride. Instead, inject typhoid–paratyphoid vaccine into an ear vein, 1 ml/5 lb. (Hold the vaccine under refrigeration when not in use. Use only adult animals because the hypothalamic heat centers are usually not fully developed in the young animal.) Obtain data as before, first under refrigeration, then at room temperature, and finally at 35°C.

A third student group should repeat the entire experiment with a control rabbit that is not injected with any drug or vaccine.

TABLE I.   Effect of Drugs upon Ability To Regulate Body Temperature

Groups	Pretreatment rectal temperatures after ½ hour adaptation	Time of post-injection reading (minutes) after additional ½ hour adaptation	Rectal temperatures		
			2°–6°C	20°C	35°C
I. Control		1. 2. 3.			
II. MgCl$_2$		1. 2. 3.			
III. Vaccine		1. 2. 3.			

Collate all the data, present them in tabular form, and draw conclusions.

Exercise 25   Secretion of Urine

Anesthetize a rabbit with sodium pentobarbital injected into an ear vein. Keep the anesthesia as light as possible to minimize blood pressure fall with subsequent slowing of kidney excretion.

Expose one vagus nerve in the neck. Cut the nerve between a proximal and distal ligature.

Expose either one internal jugular vein in the neck or else the femoral vein in the thigh. Injections are later made into the vein, either directly by needle or through a cannula placed in the vein.

Open the abdominal cavity. Locate the ureters and insert a 0.5-mm diameter catheter into each ureter. Connect the catheters by a Y-tube. After filling the catheters with saline, record the rate of drops of urine. If urine does not flow from the Y-tube after 5 minutes, inject slowly into the jugular vein 25 ml of warm saline. Determine the rate of flow.

When the rate of flow is constant, inject slowly about 25 ml of 5% urea. Redetermine the rate.

When the flow is again constant, stimulate the peripheral end of the cut vagus nerve with light alternating current from an electronic stimulator. Estimate the effect upon the pulse rate and upon the rate of urine flow.

Inject into the vein 0.5 ml of 1:10,000 epinephrine. Determine the rate of urine flow.

Inject 1 ml of phenolsulfonphthalein. Note the time of injection. Collect the urine in a beaker containing 10% sodium hydroxide. The yellow dye on mixing with alkali turns red. What was the time of initial excretion?

Certain student groups may use alternative methods for the collection of urine. One of these involves exposing the urinary bladder by a lower abdominal incision. Insert a catheter into the bladder, tying it firmly in position. Tying into the apex of the bladder is sometimes preferable to exploring for the ureters in the rabbit. Another method involves the insertion of a urethral catheter into a male rabbit without any prior surgery employed.

Rabbits should be observed and selected for urine flow beforehand inasmuch as some animals will deposit enough urinary sediment to prevent urine flow.

This is an acute, terminal experiment. Euthanatize the rabbit with an overdose of the anesthetic used.

Exercise 26   Inulin Clearance

This is a physiologic experiment involving no major surgery, but illustrating an important test of kidney function. Inulin passes freely across the glomerular membrane; it is not metabolized, does not combine with the plasma proteins, and is not excreted or resorbed by the renal tubules. Its clearance thus measures the rate of glomerular filtration.

The clearance is expressed as the volume of blood completely cleared of inulin per minute. The necessary measurements include the concentration of inulin in blood (P) and in urine (U), and also the volume of urine excreted in a unit time (V).

Above a certain magnitude of urine flow, called the *augmentation limit*, inulin excretion is maximal in the dog and man, and is not affected by further increase in urine flow. The amount of blood clearance remains constant. This is the *maximum clearance, CI*.

$$CI = \frac{UV}{P}$$

Because of the time consumed, this exercise is best undertaken as a project method, with duties divided among several student groups.

Use male rabbits weighing 2–4 kg. Feed them adequately for about a week with rabbit chow or pellets supplemented with oats and greens, and give water freely. Keep food but not water from the animals 24 hours prior to the experimental procedures. Do not anesthetize the rabbits with any long-lasting drug because of the danger of suppressing the flow of urine. Where handling becomes difficult, use thiopental or a tranquilizer.

Administer inulin by subcutaneous injection in a dose of 1 gm/kg body weight (10 ml/kg of a 10% solution). Another 5 ml may be given optionally, by ear vein, 45 minutes before the first urine-collecting period.

Two hours after the injection give the rabbit by stomach tube 5% of its body weight of warm water, and repeat the dose of water 1 hour later. One hour following the second administration of water, empty the animal's urinary bladder. This is done either by suprapubic pressure or else by using a human infant catheter for the male. The animal is then immediately placed in a metabolism cage, and urine collection periods are begun. Each period is the time from placing the animal in a cage to the time of obtaining the last drops of its urine. The several collection periods serve as checks on one another. Ordinarily, the results of each should agree.

Vary the duration of urine collection from 10 to 30 minutes, depending upon the rate of urine flow. Time with utmost accuracy the individual urine-collecting periods so that the volume flow per minute can be determined. An adequate urine volume flow is essential.

At the termination of each collection period immediately obtain 1–5 ml of blood by puncture of the femoral or marginal ear vein. Treat this blood with heparin, and centrifuge it immediately. Blood samples may be taken by heart puncture at approximately the midpoint of each urine-collection period. Plasma curves can then be constructed and plasma values obtained by interpolation to the midpoint of each urine collection period.

The chemical procedures for obtaining the concentration of inulin in plasma and urine are discussed below.

Report for an adequate urine flow the inulin clearance, in milliliters/100 gm body weight/min. Plot a graph showing clearance (in milliliters/100 gm body weight/min) as a function of urine flow (in milliliters/100 gm body weight/min). An example is shown below.

Weight of rabbit	2.5 kg
Highest rate of urine flow (V)	2.0 ml/min
Concentration of inulin in urine (U)	0.15 gm/100 ml
Concentration of inulin in plasma (P)	0.20 gm/100 ml

$$C = \frac{UV}{P}$$

or

$$\frac{0.15 \times 2.2}{0.20} = 1.65 \text{ ml/min}$$

or

$$\frac{1.65}{2.5} = 0.66 \text{ ml/kg/min} = 0.066 \text{ ml/100 gm/min}$$

Kaplan and Smith (1935) observed that the clearance of inulin in the rabbit is markedly affected by alterations in urine flow, increasing with augmentation of urine flow. This is in contrast to dogs and man. This observation was confirmed by Decker and Heller (1945). It is impossible to designate any point as an augmentation limit. The experiments in the early literature suggest that an increased water load produces an increase in the glomerular blood flow and a rise in the glomerular filtration rate.

Note that inulin for glomerular filtration rate and p-aminohippurate for effective renal plasma flow can be supplanted in laboratories using radioisotope procedures.

TECHNICAL PROCEDURE FOR INULIN IN PLASMA AND URINE

1. Principle

Inulin in the plasma or urine is hydrolyzed to fructose. The fructose is determined in a spectrophotometer at 520 μm. This is based upon a purple-violet color produced by reaction with indole-3-acetic acid in hydrochloric acid.

2. Reagents

Indole-3-acetic acid, 0.5% in ethanol. If indole-3-acetic acid is not pure white, recrystallize it from hot dilute ethanol after treatment with charcoal.

HCl, concentrated

Trichloroacetic acid, 10% aqueous

Inulin standard, 0.05 mg/ml. Dry inulin in vacuum desiccator over anhydrous $CaCl_2$ overnight. Rub 12.5 mg with 1–2 drops water in 100-ml beaker until no lumps remain. Add rapidly 50–75 ml distilled water which is nearly boiling. Rinse solution into 250 ml volumetric flask with water and dilute to volume.

3. Procedure

1. For serum or plasma, add 4.0 ml of 10% trichloroacetic acid slowly to 1.0 ml sample with mixing. Let stand 10 minutes, centrifuge, and, if necessary, filter. Urines should be diluted 1:100 with water. Sample should now contain 0.01–0.10 mg inulin per milliliter.

2. To 1.0–ml aliquots of filtrate, diluted urine, standard, and water (reagent blank), add 0.2 ml indole-3-acetic acid reagent and 8.0 ml concentrated HCl and mix.

3. Place in 37°C water bath for 75 minutes. This temperature must not be exceeded, to avoid interference from other sugars and instability of color.

4. Cool to room temperature and read absorbances of unknowns, standard, and reagent blank versus water at 520 μm. The reagent blank should have negligible absorbance. All tubes must be read rapidly since the color intensity increases approximately 0.5%/min.

3. Computations

$$\frac{\text{mg inulin}}{100 \text{ ml plasma}} = \frac{\text{unknown minus plasma blank}}{\text{standard minus reagent blank}} \times 0.05 \times 100/0.2$$

$$\frac{\text{mg inulin}}{100 \text{ ml urine}} = \frac{\text{unknown minus urine blank}}{\text{standard minus reagent blank}} \times 0.05 \times 100/0.01$$

Note that serum is interchangeable with plasma without alteration of results. Whole blood values are higher. If dextran is present in the sample, it changes the inulin values found. Remove dextran by precipitating it with ethyl alcohol.

Even if there is no inulin in normal serum, the serum blank produces a color. Part of this is due to glucose. This sugar can produce a small deviation in the results.

Exercise 27   Nephrectomy

A nephrectomy, or kidney removal, is described here employing a midline abdominal incision. Remove only the left kidney which is more readily approached than is the right kidney.

Anesthetize the rabbit with sodium pentobarbital by ear vein. Tie it down in supine position to the table. Using a No. 20 blade in a No. 4 handle, make a midline laparotomy incision starting from a point just caudal to the ensiform of the sternum and extending to a point about 3 cm below the umbilicus.

Gently push the intestines aside with sterile gauze or sponge, cut with scissors through the peritoneal covering of the kidney and, by inserting a finger, separate by blunt dissection the peritoneum from the retroperitoneal kidney and its blood vessels.

Separate the kidney, renal vessels, and ureter from the surrounding fat by blunt dissection with fingers. Use extreme caution when handling the renal vessels. Expose the kidney and lift it ventromedially. Dissect it free and then ligate the renal artery. Use 2 or 3 separate ligatures of 00 silk. (Due to the pressure in the renal artery, a figure of eight transfixation may replace the central ligature made on the renal artery.) Repeat this procedure for the renal vein. After tying the ligatures, place a hemostat on the ends of the middle and most medial ligatures. With scissors, cut between the two ligatures closest to the kidney on both the renal vein and artery. Place two ligatures on the ureter using No. 00 silk. Tie and cut between the two ligatures. Remove the kidney.

Inspect the area carefully for any bleeding. Remove the hemostats.

Closure is the same as for a laparotomy, after the single kidney has been removed.

Postoperatively, observe the animal for about two weeks and collect urine in a metabolism cage. Test the urine over this time for such changes as volume, specific gravity, and pH. Selected urine chemistry can be determined at will.

Exercise 28   Mammalian Smooth Muscle

Support a J-shaped glass rod in a beaker or muscle warmer to which a mammalian Ringer's solution is added. Place the container over a source of heat and maintain the solution at 37°C.

Euthanatize a rabbit by overanesthesia. Quickly remove the intestine, using extreme care in handling it. Immerse the excised section in cold Ringer's solution to avoid "asphyxiation." Remove a short strip, tie each end to avoid alteration of the bath by the intestinal contents, and fasten the lower end of the preparation to the short immersed part of the J-tube. Allow oxygen to bubble slowly into the preparation area continuously from a tank.

For laboratories using the classic manual apparatus, fasten the upper end of the preparation by thread to a light heart lever (Harvard Apparatus Co., Millis, Massachusetts 02054) and record the contractions on a kymograph drum (Fig. 26).

The more preferable electronic method can involve a photoelectric force transducer (myograph) in which the smooth muscle movements are transmitted from the upper end of the muscle by a loop of thread which is attached to a hook on the myograph leaf spring (Narco Bio-Systems,

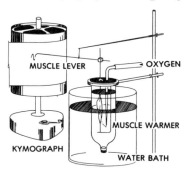

Figure 26.   Muscle preparation. Classic manual apparatus for suspending and oxygenating smooth muscle to record contractions. In the electronic method the thread from the upper end of the muscle is attached to a myograph transducer.

Houston, Texas 77017). The recording is on a channel recorder (e.g., Physiograph).

Give the preparation several minutes for spontaneous contractions to start. Adding or removing solution, which in turn alters the pressure on the intestine, occasionally stimulates contractions.

Record normal contractions, then increase the pressure on the intestine and again record contractions.

Observe the effects of raising and lowering the temperature a few degrees in each direction. Allow the preparation to adapt to each temperature selected.

Observe the effects of decreasing and then removing the oxygen supply.

Apply a moderate tetanizing current from an electronic stimulator and record the effects. Is electric current an adequate stimulus for smooth muscle?

Apply 0.5 ml of 1:40,000 epinephrine hydrochloride solution directly to the muscle.

Apply 0.5 ml of 1:40,000 pilocarpine nitrate solution.

Apply 0.5 ml of 1:40,000 atropine sulfate solution. Observe the recording for specific drug antagonism.

Do the following to show the relationship between the activity of choline and acetylcholine, and to demonstrate the protective effect of physostigmine on acetylcholine destruction:

Empty the bath; suspend a fresh strip of intestine in the container, and add fresh Ringer's solution.

Apply 0.5 ml of 1:40,000 choline chloride solution. Empty the bath and add fresh Ringer's solution.

Apply 0.5 ml of 1:100,000 acetylcholine solution. Empty the bath and add fresh Ringer's solution.

Apply 0.5 ml of 1:100,000 physostigmine salicylate solution.

Apply 0.5 ml of 1:100,000 acetylcholine solution.

Obtain a record of the effect of each drug. Indicate on the recording when each of the drugs was applied. Allow several minutes for the specific pharmacologic effect to occur.

Exercise 29 **The Machinery of Muscle Contraction**

It would be difficult to find more favorable material to study contractile tissue than the muscles of the rabbit, the muscle of choice being the psoas major, which has long straight fibers easily separated into individual units.

A. ACTOMYOSIN THREADS

Euthanatize and eviscerate a rabbit. By cutting through the lateral abdominal wall, the psoas is seen as a long, fusiform structure on the side of the lumbar region of the vertebral column. The muscle arises chiefly from lumbar vertebrae and is inserted into the femur for action on the thigh. Free the muscle, separating it along its entire length. Remove any fat grossly from the muscle tissue and place the cleaned muscle in an ice bath.

To prepare actomyosin, rapidly grind the fresh cooled muscle in a clean, chilled meat grinder with small holes. Then reduce the muscle to a pulp in an ice-cold blender.

Suspend the partly homogenized mass in cold Weber-Edsall solution ($0.6M$, KCl, $0.1\ M\ Na_2CO_3$ and $0.04\ M\ NaHCO_3$) in the ratio of 3 ml of this fluid for every gram of muscle. Stir the mass vigorously at first and then refrigerate it for 24 hours at $0°C$. Stir it occasionally during this time and more so in the final 6 hours of extraction.

A thick suspension is obtained. Strain it through cheesecloth several times until all sizable pieces of connective tissue have been removed and a homogeneous suspension containing the actomyosin remains. This is a fairly stable suspension if it is kept acid. Any dilution should be done with Weber-Edsall solution. Use only glass-distilled water in preparing the solutions used for extraction, since traces of copper can denature the protein and change the elastic property of the threads.

To produce actomyosin threads, fill an evaporating dish almost to capacity with a solution of $0.05\ M$ KCl. Draw the viscous actomyosin solution, prepared as above, into a 5-ml glass syringe with an 18-gauge needle. Dip the tip of the needle into the potassium chloride in the dish and force the actomyosin solution into the fluid. Threads should form at once.

Practice to obtain threads about 0.2 mm in diameter. Thinner ones curl and thicker ones are sluggish. Obtain 2 to 3-mm lengths. The thread consists of weakly oriented actomyosin particles. Such threads may be stored a few hours, if desired, to make them more resistant mechanically.

B. PROCEDURE

At 1 hour suck the threads cautiously and one at a time into a glass pipette. Transfer each thread to an individual watchglass containing 2–3 ml of $0.1\ M$ KCl solution. Measure the length of the thread. Then add several drops of of 0.1–0.2% adenosine triphosphate (ATP) to the medium, and again measure the length of the thread. Squirt the ATP in to reach the thread from all sides. Add a few drops of 2.0 M KCl and observe any changes.

The expected results indicate that contraction involves a change in actomyosin, caused by interaction with ATP. Salts are essential to the process. This experiment recapitulates the historic achievement of Szent-Gyorgi in helping to explain physicochemical events in muscle contraction.

If there is no evidence of contraction of the threads, add 0.001 M or 0.002 M MgCl$_2$ to the evaporating dish containing the 0.05 M KCl solution and into which the actomyosin is to be squirted. Magnesium promotes gelation.

In the original procedure described above to extract actomyosin from muscle, it is possible to obtain the globulin, myosin, rather than actomyosin, although the latter is the form in which myosin is thought to exist in the myofibril.

To obtain myosin, alter the procedure so that the muscle is extracted with 0.5 M KCl solution, for only 15 minutes. The myosin is then precipitated by excessive dilution with distilled water. The resulting decrease of the ionic strength favors the precipitation of the myosin.

If an insufficient quantity of actomyosin is obtained because only the psoas muscle is used, then it is best to remove the skin of the rabbit and strip as many of the underlying muscles as possible. The fresh, defatted muscles from one rabbit can yield up to 300 gm of ground tissue.

C. ADENOSINE TRIPHOSPHATE

ATP is most readily obtained commercially, but it may also be obtained in fresh boiled muscle extract. While removing the psoas, mince the rest of the body muscle, suspend it in an equal volume of boiling water, and quickly heat the material to 80°–100°C. Strain and press the mass through a cloth, then use the extract.

Exercise 30 **The Autonomic Nervous System: The Cervical Sympathetic Nerve**

Use an albino rabbit in this exercise where circulation in the ears must be visualized. Closely shave the ears of the rabbit, taking care not to injure the vessels or the nerves. Do not wet or handle the ears excessively thereafter.

Anesthetize the animal with sodium pentobarbital followed by an inhalant anesthetic if necessary. Isolate on one side the carotid artery sheath and three delicate nerves. The vagus nerve is the largest and the depressor nerve is the smallest. The cervical sympathetic nerve is identified by tetanizing it with weak shocks from a stimulator and observing the size of the pupil or the blood vessels of the ear on the same side as the nerve stimulated. Keep all cervical tissues moistened with warm Ringer's solution.

Place a loose ligature about the cervical sympathetic nerve after separating it from the vagus nerve. Position the ligature about one-half inch below the cricoid cartilage. Contrast the changes in pupillary diameter of the two eyes and also contrast the changes in the vascular diameters of the two ears upon tying the ligature tightly, and shortly thereafter.

Cut the cervical sympathetic nerve below the ligature. Compare the appearance of the blood vessels of the two ears by holding a light behind the ears. Do the two ears have a different temperature?

Hold a light behind the ear on the side where the cervical sympathetic was cut. Raise the nerve gently and stimulate it above the ligature with tetanizing current. What changes occur in the blood vessels of the ear? Observe also on the ipsilateral side, during stimulation, the diameter of the pupil, the position of the nictitating membrane, the width of the palpebral fissure, and the position of the eyeball independent of any change in the width of the palpebral fissure.

Compare the effects after section of the nerve but without stimulation with those observed during nerve stimulation.

Expose the nerves on the other side of the neck. Trace the cervical sympathetic nerve up to the highest (cranial) cervical ganglion. Observe the pupil while applying 1% nicotine solution to the ganglion. Stimulate the preganglionic fibers (caudal to the ganglion) and observe the pupil and the ear vessels. Repeat the observations while stimulating the postganglionic fibers (proceeding cranially from the ganglion).

This is an acute exercise. Euthanatize the rabbit with an overdose of the barbiturate.

Exercise 31   **The Autonomic Nervous System:
The Depressor Nerve**

Anesthetize a rabbit with sodium pentobarbital plus inhalant anesthetics if needed. Isolate the vagus nerves on both sides of the neck, and the depressor nerve and the carotid artery on only one side.

Insert a cannula into the carotid artery and connect it with a mechanical or, preferably, an electronic system to record blood pressure. The mean carotid blood pressure of the anesthetized rabbit is about 95 torr. Heparin may be employed as an anticoagulant. Sodium citrate (10%), although used for dogs, is not a suitable anticoagulant for rabbits. Have a marker in the circuit to record time events.

Gently raise the depressor nerve and stimulate it with weak tetanizing current above a ligature previously placed loosely around the nerve. Record any changes in the resting blood pressure. What is the effect upon the heart rate?

Tie another ligature around the depressor nerve, tighten both ligatures and cut the nerve between the two ligatures. Stimulate the end of the nerve nearer the heart, and record any effect upon blood pressure while observing any change in the heart rate. Then stimulate the end away from the heart and compare the effects.

Place two ligatures around each vagus nerve. Cut each nerve between the ligatures, avoiding traction on these nerves. Replace the nerve stumps in the wound and cover them with moist warm cotton. When the blood pressure attains a constant level, find the depressor nerve again and stimulate the end of the depressor nerve away from the heart. Determine the blood pressure and heart rate before and after stimulation and compare them with the corresponding values before the vagi were cut. Discuss the function of the depressor nerve.

This exercise can be simplified if desired by recording blood pressure with a sphygmomanometer, thus eliminating carotid cannulation and the transduction amplifying/recording instruments.

This is an acute exercise. Euthanatize the rabbit with an overdose of the barbiturate.

Exercise 32 **Anatomy of the Central Nervous System**

This exercise involves an anatomic dissection and exploration designed specifically to facilitate the next two exercises. Euthanatize a rabbit and position it so that the dorsal surface is upward (ventral recumbency or prone). Secure the rabbit to the surgical table. Incise and retract the skin and underlying fascia of the cranial region. Open the bony skull, using caution not to damage the brain. Use a mechanical trephine or an electric drill and enlarge the holes with a Rongeur forceps. Observe the cerebral meninges and then remove them.

In the exposed dorsal view the *cerebral hemispheres* are seen directly below the incisions. They are the most prominent structures of the entire brain and they extend backward to cover most of the other structures of

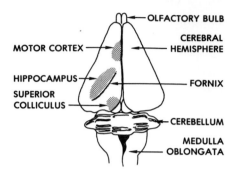

Figure 27. Dorsal brain anatomy. Dorsal aspect of the rabbit brain. The position of the motor cortex, hippocampus, and superior colliculus is indicated by the shaded areas.

the brain. The cortex, which is the external part of the cerebrum, is mildly folded into gyri and sulci. Slice inward to observe the inner whitish medulla. Observe that the paired hemispheres of the cortex are divided by the median longitudinal cerebral fissure (Fig. 27).

The *olfactory bulbs* are a pair of protrusions cranial to each cerebral hemisphere.

The *cerebellum* is just caudal to the cerebral hemispheres. Its surface seems to have several lobes. Its outer cortical surface is increased by foliations rather than by foldings to gyri and sulci.

The *optic lobes,* or *corpora quadrigemina,* lie in the median plane, between the cerebrum and the cerebellum. They are the dorsal parts of the midbrain.

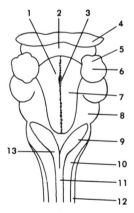

Figure 28. Dorsal hindbrain anatomy. Dorsal view of the hindbrain with cerebellum removed: (1) Medial eminence, (2) anterior medullary velum, (3) dorsal median fissure, (4) caudal colliculus, (5) brachium conjunctivum, (6) brachium pontis, (7) rhomboid fossa, (8) brachium ad medullam, (9) clava, (10) column of Burdach, (11) dorsal median sulcus, (12) dorsal lateral sulcus, and (13) column of Goll.

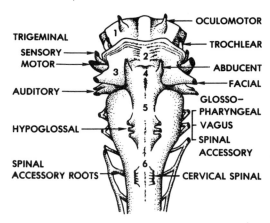

Figure 29.   Ventral hindbrain anatomy. Ventral view of the hindbrain. The cerebellar attachments have been removed. (1) Cerebral peduncle, (2) pons, (3) trapezoid body, (4) foramen cecum, (5) pyramid, and (6) ventral median fissure.

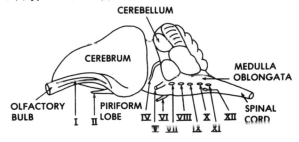

Figure 30.   Brain anatomy, longitudinal. External longitudinal view of the rabbit brain. The cranial nerves are almost all visible in this view and are designated by Roman numerals. The cerebrum covers the diencephalon and mesencephalon only, and its cortex is smooth. The olfactory bulbs are prominent. The pons is not conspicuous.

The *hindbrain* in its more cranial section includes the cerebellum above and the pons below (Fig. 28). The *medulla oblongata* forms the entire caudal aspect of the hindbrain. The medulla provides a pathway for ascending and descending tracts as well as an area in which many vital centers are located. Most of the cranial nerves will be seen leaving the medulla on either side. Identify these nerves (Fig. 29).

If time permits, remove the brain and identify its substructures in lateral and medial views (Figs. 30 and 31).

THE VERTEBRAL COLUMN

The vertebral column of the rabbit is made up of 46 vertebrae; the usual vertebral formula is $C_7T_{12}L_7S_4C_{16}$. Identify the regions of the

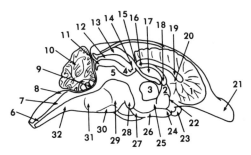

Figure 31. Brain anatomy, medial longitudinal. Medial longitudinal view of the rabbit brain. (1) Cerebrum, (2) anterior commissure, (3) thalamus, (4) thalamus, (5) cerebral aqueduct, (6) central canal of spinal cord, (7) fourth ventricle, (8) posterior medullary velum, (9) anterior medullary velum, (10) cerebellum, (11) inferior colliculus, (12) superior colliculus, (13) pineal gland, (14) habenula, (15) choroid plexus over third ventricle, (16) splenium, (17) hippocampus, (18) fornix, (19) corpus callosum, (20) septum pellucidum, (21) olfactory bulb, (22) lamina terminalis, (23) optic nerve, (24) optic chiasm, (25) area of third ventricle, (26) tuber cinereum, (27) infundibulum, (28) mammillary body, (29) cerebral peduncle, (30) pons, (31) medulla oblongata, and (32) cervical flexure.

spine and locate the sections by superficial palpation. The caudal nine coccygeal vertebrae do not have arches and cannot be easily felt. Make a midline incision over the spinous process of the lumbar vertebra and dissect away all muscles and fascia. Note the ease of movement of the exposed vertebral column. Make bilateral cuts through the bone between the articular processes and the spinous processes, using a dental drill or small bone saw. Remove the dorsal section of a vertebra to expose the spinal cord covered by its meninges.

The three meningeal membranes are the dura mater, arachnoidea, and pia mater. The spinal dura mater is separated from the periosteum of the enclosing vertebrae by the epidural space, which is occupied by fat and blood vessels. The subdural space is the cavity between the dura mater and the arachnoidea. The arachnoidea is a delicate, transparent membrane which forms the outer wall of the subarachnoid space. This space contains the cerebrospinal fluid. The spinal pia mater is the innermost meninx and it intimately covers the spinal cord. The outer layer of the pia mater is fibrous tissue. The inner layer is vascular and adheres to the spinal cord.

Exercise 33   **Motor Areas of the Cerebrum**

Anesthetize a rabbit with sodium pentobarbital. Add an inhalation anesthetic by face cone if needed, lightening the depth of anesthesia when stimulating the cerebral cortex. If narcosis is too deep, muscle contractions in response to cortical stimulation may not occur.

Incise and retract the skin and fascia of the scalp. Open the skull over one hemisphere with a mechanical or electrical trephine. Drill several holes and enlarge the opening with Rongeur forceps. Keep all exposed tissue moistened with warm Ringer-Locke's solution.

Although care must be taken in the midline region because of the possibility of cutting into the venous sinuses, it is, nevertheless, feasible to work in the midline since the underlying dura may be left intact by careful manipulation and very little bleeding may be expected from these sinuses.

To stop oozing of blood from the diploe, press warm bone wax against the bleeding zones. The wax can be obtained commercially or else made up as a mixture of 1 part of beeswax to 3 parts of paraffin. Cut through the dura mater and reflect it. Identify the central fissure.

Suspend the rabbit in a canvas hammock with four holes cut in it so that the rabbit's legs hang freely, which allows ready observation of movements. Stimulate various areas in the motor cortex with weak tetanizing shocks of controlled frequency from a stimulator. Note the positions of the cerebral areas causing responses in various voluntary muscles. Observe the muscles involved, the degree of coordination, and the extensiveness of the responses. Note whether responses are contralateral to the cerebrum.

Place a few crystals of strychnine nitrate on the pial surface of the cerebral area controlling the movements of the foreleg. Observe after 10 to 40 minutes muscular tremors followed by twitching of the neck and limbs. The seizure is of an epileptoid nature, involving first one set of muscles, then a spread or march of the disturbance, as in an attack of Jacksonian epilepsy.

The student is referred to an early paper by Allen (1931) showing areas of the rabbit brain that may be selected for electrical stimulation with ordinary bipolar electrodes. Allen used an induction coil with a 2-/to 3-volt battery source. Electronic stimulators were not then available.

The following summarizes the localized responses to be expected.

1. *Motor areas.* With strong faradic current the pulse and respiratory rate decrease. With very strong current tonic spasms and clonic convulsions occur.

2. *Superior colliculus.* With weak faradic current the pulse rate increases and there are generalized muscle spasms. With strong current the pulse is slow but strong.

3. *Olfactory areas.* With weak faradic current there are no observable changes in the pulse or respiration. With strong current the responses resemble those from stimulation of the motor areas.

4. *Hippocampus.* Expose this area by removing an overlying cortical

strip of tissue in a superoposterior segment of one hemisphere. Weak faradic current produces no visible change in the pulse or respiration. Strong current produces responses resembling those from stimulation of the motor areas.

Exercise 34   **Hemilaminectomy**

The dorsal arch extends upward from the body of a vertebra and leaves a space called the vertebral foramen between the arch and the body. The foramen provides a protective case for the spinal cord.

The dorsal arch and vertebral body carry the processes of the vertebrae, including articular, transverse, and spinous processes. The surgery selected in the present exercise involves removal of one half of the arch including its lamina. Each group may select a different lumbar vertebra for the operation.

A. PROCEDURE

Anesthetize a rabbit with sodium pentobarbital, supplemented with an inhalant anesthetic if necessary. Tie the animal down in prone position (ventral recumbency) on the surgical table. Use aseptic technique, all instruments and materials being previously autoclaved.

Make a midline incision dorsally over the length of the lumbar spine. Incise the deep fascia to expose the deep erector spinae group of muscles. By bluntly dissecting away the muscle fibers, expose the dorsal arch of one or more lumbar vertebrae. Displace all muscle by packing it to one side.

Carefully remove the bony processes over one or more intervertebral spaces. Removal can be done manually with a Rongeur forceps and trephine, although electric drills with tiny bits are more satisfactory. Control bleeding in the deep fascial areas. Clear the region for better visualization by syringing it with warm, sterile, isotonic saline solution.

Elevate the root of a nerve in the intervertebral space. Identify the accompanying blood vessels and ligate such vessels.

Test whether the spinal cord is intact. Electrically stimulate a nerve at its exit from the cord and observe whether there is movement of the limbs.

Transect the nerve roots with scissors. Test the immediate effects of denervation.

To close the wound, bring together the deep structures with No. 00 chromic catgut. Close the skin edges with interrupted, nonabsorbable sutures.

B. POSTSURGICAL TESTING

The hemilaminectomized rabbit may require exercise of limbs, and possibly bladder catheterization and enemas.

In animals that recover well, test after a few weeks for motor function in respect to any local or generalized abnormal body posture, equilibrium, and righting reactions.

Test for normal and abnormal sensory functions by evaluating pain and pressure responses through the body as well as locally.

Test for the presence of the knee kick and for several of the tendon reflexes.

Note especially whether the losses correspond to the level of the neural structures that were transected.

If the rabbit shows signs of paralysis, it should be immediately euthanatized.

Exercise 35   **Resection of the Jejunum Using an End-to-End Anastomosis**

This exercise is to provide surgical experience for a team consisting of a surgeon, anesthetist, and technician/recorder.

Anesthetize a rabbit with sodium pentobarbital, using supplementary anesthesia if needed. Place the animal in supine position and secure it to the surgical table.

Make an incision, about 6½ cm (2½ inches) long, extending longitudinally over most of the left rectus abdominis muscle in the ventral abdominal wall. Incise the peritoneum to expose the visceral organs.

Select a section of the jejunum to be resected and lift it ventrally to find all blood vessels entering it. Put tight ligatures around every observable vessel. Incise the mesenteries to clear the area.

Place intestinal clamps across the proximal and distal ends of the selected jejunal section so that at least 5 cm of the jejunum are thus enclosed. With a scalpel cut out the intestinal section between the clamps. The field is then ready for anastomosis (Fig. 32A).

Use a very fine straight needle and fine suture material (e.g., silk) to anastomose the cut ends of the intestine. Use interrupted Lembert sutures. To do this, pass the needle and suture twice in a straight line through the same side of the tissue (Fig. 32B). Then pass the suture material across the gap, and again pass it twice through the opposite cut end of the jejunum. Bring the free loops together, but do not tie them. Repeat this suturing procedure with several independent stitches placed close together. Do not tie any of them.

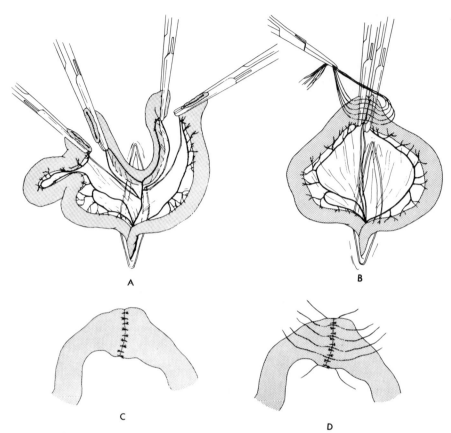

Figure 32. End-to-end anastomosis. (A) Incising bowel, (B) inverting closure with Lembert, (C) completed Lembert, and (D) Lembert overlay.

When the sutures have been placed on one side, rotate the clamps that were previously positioned on the cut ends of the jejunum. This brings the opposite face of the jejunum into view. Similarly approximate the cut ends on that face with interrupted Lembert sutures. Each of the two groups of sutures is held as a unit in each needle holder. Remove the clamps which were originally placed on each side of the cut.

Tie the sutures, one at a time, on each side of the jejunum. These sutures permit a wide area to be approximated and simultaneously the free edges are inverted (Fig. 32C).

Place a small number of Lembert sutures to form a second row to reinforce the first row (Fig. 32D). Test the anastomosed ends to see that the intestinal lumen is patent.

Close the abdominal wall with simple, interrupted, nonabsorbable sutures. Treat the rabbit with antibiotics because of the high risk of peritonitis.

Observe the rabbit postoperatively, providing it with ample, clean drinking water, but no food by mouth for 24 hours, followed by small feedings every 8 hours for the next 48 hours.

Exercise 36 **Thyroidectomy**

To excise the rabbit thyroid gland, a historic procedure is still valid (Tatum, 1913).

Each group should assign division of responsibilities to a surgeon, anesthetist, and technician/recorder. Tie down the rabbit in supine position. Work aseptically and use sodium pentobarbital as the primary anesthetic. Make a median incision about 5 cm long in the ventral aspect of the neck of the rabbit. Center the incision over the prominence of the larynx. With fine-pointed forceps, free the inferior pole of the thyroid gland from the laryngeal nerve in that area, and then isolate the thyroid gland upward. Either ligate the single thyroid artery before division or crush it with forceps until the clotting of blood within it permits its division without ligation. The latter method is more satisfactory in young rabbits since they have smaller arteries.

Follow the deeper cranial pole of the gland laterally and cranially until its sheath is exposed, and then separate it from the connective tissue. Free the median superior attachment from the thyroid cartilage. Reflect this lobe together with the connecting isthmus over the remaining lobe and separate the latter in a similar manner. This frees the thyroid gland. The rabbits are then essentially cretins, although the completeness of thyroid removal may not be fully known at operation.

Do not disturb the external pair of parathyroid glands, which are usually observable. They lie lateral, but occasionally caudal, to and separate from the thyroid lobes.

The cretin rabbits should be observed for several weeks. Record several gross observations before and after thyroidectomy, including body weight, appetite, general vigor, dryness and fullness of the hair, and degree of abdominal distention.

Determine the blood cholesterol (1) before operation; (2) when symptoms occur postoperatively; (3) after a period of feeding desiccated thyroid. The blood cholesterol in the cretins should be greater than normal, decreasing with the feeding of thyroid preparations. In laboratories working with radioisotopes, this exercise lends itself well to the study of uptake of radioisotopes of iodine in the cretin.

BLOOD CHOLESTEROL DETERMINATION

The blood should be allowed to clot and determinations made, preferably on fresh serum. Analyses can be performed readily in automated instruments for blood chemistry. There are several commercial models available and directions accompany each instrument. The classic methods using a spectrophometer can give precise results, but they are tedious.

Exercise 37   **The Pancreatic Hormone**

The exercise demonstrates the effect of insulin on the blood sugar. Take a 2-ml sample of blood for a sugar determination from the marginal ear vein of a 2-kg rabbit that has been starved for 24 hours. Then inject subcutaneously 80 units of insulin to obtain an observable effect. Some of the signs of hypoglycemia are hyperirritablility, convulsions, and coma.

A second blood sample is drawn as soon as distress is evident, and a third when the animal begins to display convulsions.

To relieve the induced hypoglycemia, inject 50 ml of 10% glucose intravenously. After recovery take another blood sample for sugar determination. It usually takes several injections of glucose to control the hypoglycemia that has developed.

Compare the blood sugar values in all samples. Determine the blood sugar with a photoelectric colorimeter, spectrophotometer, or with commercial automated instruments. Directions for operation are supplied with the photoelectric automated instruments. The normal blood sugar values in a rabbit range from about 80 to 110 mg/100 ml of blood.

Use a No. 25 gauge needle for central or marginal ear veins. If blood is taken by cardiac puncture, use a No. 18 gauge needle having a 1½-/inch stem length.

DETERMINATION OF BLOOD SUGAR BY A PHOTOELECTRIC METHOD

1. Reagents for Blood Sugar

Sulfuric acid, 0.66 N (standard volumetric solution)
Sodium tungstate, 10%
Alkaline copper tartrate reagent (Folin and Wu)
Phosphomolybdic acid reagent (Folin and Wu)

2. Protein-Free Blood Filtrate

Into a flask place 2 ml of oxalated blood plus 14 ml of distilled water. Use saturated sodium oxalate, 0.1 ml to 5 ml of blood.

Add slowly to this blood, 2 ml of 10% sodium tungstate. Rotate the flask while adding this. Avoid foam. Add 2 ml of 0.66 N sulfuric acid and rotate the flask gently.

Mix everything thoroughly. The coagulum should be dark brown with no frothing. If the coagulum is brownish-pink there is usually too much oxalate. If so, add 10% sulfuric acid, one drop at a time, shaking vigorously after each drop until there is no foaming and the dark brown color appears.

Filter through Whatman No. 40 paper. The filtrate should be clear and colorless. Do not filter over 10 minutes, otherwise the evaporation error will be considerable. As an alternative, the material may be centrifuged and the clear supernate used.

Into a Folin-Wu sugar tube place 2 ml of tungstic acid filtrate and 2 ml of alkaline copper tartrate. Mix by lateral shaking. Place in a boiling water bath for exactly 8 minutes and then cool in running water. Mix by vigorous lateral shaking. Add 2 ml of phosphomolybdic acid reagent and place in a boiling water bath for 5 minutes. Dilute to the 20-ml graduation. Mix by repeated inversion and shaking and transfer to an absorption cell. Read in a photoelectric colorimeter with the appropriate filter (630 mμ in place, or read in a spectrophotometer. Determine the concentration in milligrams/100 ml of whole blood from a previously calibrated graph.

3. The Calibration Curve

Prepare a glucose standard solution. Dissolve 1.0 gm of anhydrous D-glucose in 100 ml of 0.25% benzoic acid, to make a 1% solution. Dilute 0.1, 0.2, 0.3, 0.4, 0.5 ml, etc., of the stock standard to 24 ml with 0.25% benzoic acid. Each milliliter of the working standards contains 0.04 mg, 0.08 mg, 0.12 mg, 0.16 mg, 0.2 mg, and higher.

To establish the calibration curve, add 2 ml of alkaline copper tartrate reagent to 2.0 ml of each of the working standards in a Folin-Wu sugar tube. Place in boiling water for 6 minutes. Place in cold water without agitation for 3 minutes. Add 2 ml of phosphomolybdic acid reagent and let stand at room temperature for 2 minutes and then dilute to the 25-ml graduation with diluted phosphomolybdic acid (1 part to 4 parts of water). Mix by repeated inversion and transfer the solution to an absorption cell.

Read in an instrument that has been previously set for 100 % transmission and at the appropriate wavelength. In doing this, use a blank that has been treated in exactly the same way as in the above procedure, except that it contains neither blood nor sugar.

To obtain the curve, plot the values obtained from the standard solution. Using semilog paper, plot transmission values on the logarithmic scale against concentration on the linear scale. The curve may also be obtained by plotting the log of the readings against concentration or its equivalent in terms of milligrams/100 ml of blood. (Concentration in milligrams/100 ml serum equals 500 / milligrams/2 ml working standard.)

Exercise 38   Simulation of Pancreatectomy by Alloxan

The operative removal of the diffuse pancreas is highly troublesome in the rabbit. Alloxan provides a ready means for pharmacologically depancreatizing the rabbit by its selective necrosing action on the beta cells of the islets of Langerhans. The degree of damage after a given dose varies considerably. There may be some damage to the liver and kidneys. As early as 1937, Jacobs had noted the effect of alloxan in rabbits, that is, an initial hyperglycemia and a subsequent hypoglycemia. The diabetic condition results from failure of the secreting cells to produce insulin, whereas the hypoglycemia results possibly from liver damage or else from insulin secreted excessively by the injured islets. The hyperglycemia occurs in the acute phase, although this phase may not appear. The hypoglycemia is characteristic and constant.

Take a 2-ml sample of blood for a control sugar determination from the marginal ear vein of a young adult rabbit that has fasted for 12–24 hours. Determine the blood sugar by the procedure stated in the previous exercise dealing with the pancreatic hormone.

Prepare an aqueous 10 % alloxan solution containing 100 mg/ml and inject it intravenously in a dose of 1 ml (100 mg)/kg body weight.

Collect blood samples at 1 hour, 2 hours, 4 hours, and at 24 hours after injection. Determine the blood sugar in each sample, and plot a curve of blood sugar (in milligrams/100 ml) against time (in hours).

Observe the initial transient hyperglycemia and the subsequent hypoglycemia that begins in 3–4 hours and continues to fall until the animal dies. Note the convulsive sugar level (less than 35 mg of glucose/100 ml of blood).

The convulsions and hyperglycemia can be relieved quickly by intravenous injection of glucose. When the acute effects of alloxan have subsided, the rabbit returns rapidly to a normal state.

Exercise 39   **Adrenalectomy**

It has been claimed (controversially) by early investigators (Firor and Grollman, 1933) that the rabbit is an animal in which the widespread occurrence of accessory cortical tissue, in at least 25% of all cases, allows indefinite survival after adrenalectomy. Firor and Grollman asserted that survival is a result of regeneration of tissue remaining at the operative site, chiefly along the caudal vena cava.

The following exercise illustrates the essential surgical excision procedure and emphasizes some of the functions of the adrenal glands.

Do not feed the rabbit for 48 hours prior to the operative procedure, otherwise the adrenal glands may be obscured by the distended loops of intestine.

Use sodium pentobarbital as the primary anesthetic agent. Anesthesia should be deep enough to suppress movement because of the possibility of the tearing of blood vessels during the search for and removal of the glands. The adrenal glands are ordinarily located medial and anterior to the kidneys. They are light in color, elliptical, and readily observable by the unaided eyes.

Make a high rectus incision about 5 cm long directly in the midline of the abdominal wall. Expose the left adrenal gland and incise its peritoneal coat. With fine-tipped forceps bring ligatures around the blood vessels passing in and out of the gland. Tie the ligatures tightly and divide the blood vessels between them. Remove the adrenal gland. Following removal of the gland watch closely for signs of bleeding before turning away from the operative site. Do not attempt to repair the connective tissues that were removed to clear the field.

If desired, repeat the manipulations to excise the right adrenal gland. It may be necessary to tie off a section of the vena cava with firm ligatures.

It may be advisable not to excise both glands since the severe changes that ensue will complicate the replacement therapy needed. Excision of one adrenal can suffice to illustrate the surgical technique. Bilateral removal necessitates a midline rather than a paramedian abdominal incision. In clearing the field, keep the intestines to one side with sterile, saline-moistened gauze or sponges.

In closing the abdominal cavity, suture the peritoneum and muscle with No. 00 medium chromic gut. Finally, approximate the edges of the skin with individual sutures. Vetafil is satisfactory for the external suturing. For bilateral adrenalectomy each group should operate upon two rabbits, because of the high operative risk of death.

Follow the progress of the animals daily during their period of survival. Without intensive care bilaterally adrenalectomized rabbits usually survive up to 10 days. Make a record of some of the signs of adrenal insufficiency, including restlessness, weight loss, weakness, drop in body temperature, hypotension, and anorexia. The animals show a liability to suffer death from minor environmental causes. If laboratory data are desired, draw 5 ml of blood several days postoperatively and centrifuge it to obtain serum. Make determinations of glucose, sodium, potassium, and chloride.

Exercise 40   **Hypophysectomy: Intraorbital Approach**

The hypophysis is necessary for ovulation, the life of the corpus luteum, and implantation of the embryo. If the hypophysis is excised, ovulation and corpora lutea formation are suppressed.

The rabbit corpus luteum is acted upon by hypophyseal hormones indirectly. The hormone probably directly responsible for corpus luteum maintenance in the rabbit is estrogen from the ovarian follicles. Thus, in the absence of the hypophyseal support, estrogen is not synthesized and secreted and the corpus luteum regresses. If the hypophysis is removed before implantation, in addition to the lack of corpus luteum formation the ova will not implant due to the lack of proper oviductal and uterine hormonal support.

Remove the hypophysis 3 days after copulation. Do a laparotomy at any interval from 4 to 10 days postcopulation *or* after the hypophysectomy. In comparison with a normal pregnant animal, the corpora lutea will be seen to be regressed and the ovaries atrophied. Implantation may have begun, but the pregnancy will not continue.

PROCEDURE

Several methods have been developed to hypophysectomize a rabbit. Fee and Parkes (1929) described a partial decerebration in which the frontal part of the parietal and temporal lobes of the brain were removed. This operation was too severe, and the animals survived only 24 hours.

There is a procedure in the early literature (Firor, 1933) in which a rabbit can be hypophysectomized by an intraorbital approach to the sella turcica, or bony saddle in which the pituitary gland lies. The directions below follow his approach.

1. Inject sodium pentobarbital into an ear vein, and follow with an inhalant anesthetic as needed.

2. Elevate the animal's head and turn the head and thorax to one side.

3. Enlarge the palpebral fissure with a lateral incision starting just below the temporal canthus and with a medial incision extending one cm from the nasal canthus.

4. Retract the flap constituting the lower lid. Then divide the palpebral conjunctiva. This exposes the ligament bridging the posterior half of the zygomatic arch, part of which forms the infraorbital ridge.

5. Split and excise this ligament. To provide adequate operative space in the orbit, grasp and excise the underlying fat.

6. Incise the tissues attached to the medial end of the supraorbital process. This exposes the abrupt end of this part of the frontal bone.

7. Insert a spatula into the deepest part of the orbit. Bring it forward to compress the orbital sinus, which is a venous sinus covering the posterior half of the eye. The eye can then be delivered without significant bleeding. If any hemorrhage does occur, pack the orbital cavity for a few minutes with gauze.

8. With the eye held out of the orbit, remove areolar tissue and fat covering the fifth cranial nerve. The nerve merges along the medial edge of the internal pterygoid muscle. Stop any bleeding with gauze and mild pressure.

9. Puncture the thin lateral wall of the sella turcica which lies behind the internal pterygoid muscle. To do this, place a straight forceps in the groove at the medial edge of the superior border of the fifth nerve under the edge of the pterygoid muscle until the forceps reaches the bony wall of the orbit. The bone is broken by exerting slight pressure on the forceps. Enlarge the aperture by opening and rotating the forceps. Remove any blood by aspiration.

10. Try to remove the pituitary gland by applying suction through a beveled-ended glass tube inserted into the sella. Exert great care to have the bevel of the tube facing away from the pituitary stalk (infundibulum) or else the suction applied to the base of the brain may injure or kill the animal.

11. Withdraw the glass tube, lift out the spatula, and replace the eye in the orbit. Close each incision with a single suture. No dressing need be applied to the eye.

Firor found that removal of the hypophysis 35 minutes after copulation prevented ovulation. This was seen by examining the ovaries a few days later. Hypophysectomy 3 days after copulation caused regression of the corpora lutea, ovarian atrophy, and termination of pregnancy, as seen in a laparotomy performed a few days after the hypophysectomy.

The present writers find this operation to be difficult for the beginning student and recommend that the same steps should first be performed in a euthanatized rabbit.

Smith and White (1931) hypophysectomized rabbits by an oral approach. The soft palate was incised, and the large blood sinus around the pituitary gland was injected with warm bone wax. The dense capsule surrounding the gland was exposed and opened and the entire pituitary gland was removed by suction into a cannula. In this operation all structures were visible, bleeding was minimal, recovery was fast, and the animals survived for variable periods of time.

The writers of the present text recommend a modified transsphenoidal approach which is described in the next exercise.

Exercise 41   **Hypophysectomy: Ventral Cervical Approach**

Rabbit skulls should be available to study the landmarks and the exact direction of approach to be made.

Anesthetize the rabbit with sodium pentobarbital and tie it down to the surgical table in supine position. Shave the ventral neck skin and clean the area with soap and water followed by 2% iodine.

Make a longitudinal incision in the ventral neck starting at the level of the thyroid gland and running up almost to the symphysis of the mandible. Reflect the salivary glands to each side, separate the tracheal muscles, and expose the trachea. Retract the trachea, esophagus, and tracheal muscles, exposing the base of the skull. In retracting the trachea, be careful not to produce an occlusion.

Place retractors around the area to provide good visual exposure. Clean the surface of the basal skull by blunt dissection, working gradually inward.

Set up certain landmarks of approach. If the mandible is about parallel to the surface of the table, establish a line about 1 cm in front of the angle of the mandible. The direction of penetration should be perpendicular to the center of this line.

Use a dental drill or a drill with a smooth shaft and burr tip. A threaded shaft will entangle and destroy structures through which it penetrates. The tip of the fine bit should travel about 3 cm before it reaches the basisphenoid bone. The bit then meets the bone at an angle. Tilt the drill about 20° anteriorly. Carefully perforate the bone. A slight "give" is felt as the drill goes just through the bone.

The pituitary gland should be directly under the site of entry. The gland is not visible at this stage. Remove the gland by strong suction. This is readily accomplished through a fine pipette attached to the vacuum line of a water aspirator. Aspirate blood in the field. Flush the area with warm sterile saline.

Remove the retractors and repair the cervical deep tissue and skin wound. Give 10% glucose solution in the early postoperative period.

After a week or so, study the behavioral characteristics of the rabbit and look for any signs of pituitary deficiency.

When observations have been completed, necropsy the euthanatized rabbit. Examine the skull to confirm the prior destruction of the pituitary gland.

Exercise 42 Ovariohysterectomy

This exercise requires a review of the anatomy of the female rabbit genital tract prior to operation. It provides experience in a survival surgical procedure. A wide variation should be anticipated in the appearance, location, and condition of the uterine horns and ovaries, depending on the age, sexual stage, and the number of previous litters.

Sterilize all instruments, cotton, gauze, and sutures. Include scalpel, forceps, scissors, hemostats, retractors, needle holder, and suture needles.

Anesthetize a nonpregnant female rabbit by injecting very slowly 1 ml/kg body weight of a 5.0% sodium pentobarbital solution (50 mg/kg), into an ear vein. If necessary, supplement the barbiturate with an inhalant anesthetic administered by nasal cone.

Tie the rabbit in supine position to a surgical table and elevate its head end. Using scissors and electric animal clippers, remove an area of hair 6 cm wide, beginning at the pubic symphysis and extending the epilation about 8 cm forward. Follow this by shaving the hair with a razor. Clean the operative site with soap and warm water, followed by 70% alcohol and then 2% iodine.

With the head still elevated, express urine from the animal by firm pressure applied in a dorsocaudal direction upon the lower abdomen. Repeat this maneuver until the urine flow stops from the compressed urinary bladder.

Reverse the tilt of the surgical table so that the hind part of the rabbit is elevated. This displaces the digestive organs in a cranial direction, thus allowing easier access to the genital tract.

From a point in the midline about 2 cm cranial to the pubic symphysis, make a skin incision that extends 5 cm forward. Retract each edge of the incised skin toward its own side. Expose the viscera by a single midline incision through both the abdominal muscles and the peritoneum. Use retractors to obtain a clear view of the abdominal organs. Identify the empty urinary bladder. Observe the uterine horns on either side of the bladder as they travel longitudinally along the body wall.

Hook one of the horns with a retractor or tenaculum and gently bring the horn into view. With firm traction pull the ovary into the operative field. In a young rabbit take special caution since the fragile structures may tear. Place two hemostats on the pedicle cranial to the ovary, and tie a ligature in front of the more cranial hemostat. Chromic catgut, size 00, is satisfactory for internal ligatures and sutures employed here. Separate the ovary and horn from the pedicle by cutting with a scalpel between the hemostats. Holding the ends of the tied ligature, release the more cranial hemostat on the pedicle. If hemorrhage does not occur, cut the ligature ends short and let the pedicle stump slip back into the abdomen. Leave the other hemostat clamped to the ovary and its horn to prevent oozing of blood into the field. Cut the mesentery (mesometrium) along the horn caudally to control bleeding. The uterine body represents the caudal area of fusion of the paired horns. Repeat the same procedure to free the opposite ovary and its horn.

With hemostats on each horn, apply gentle traction and pull the body of the uterus in a cranial direction so that it comes into clearer view. Place two additional hemostats across the uterine body being careful to clamp cranial to the urethra. Anchor a ligature to the body of the uterus with a stitch; then bring its ends around the uterus caudal to the hemostats on the uterine body, making sure that the ligature also surrounds the uterine artery and vein. Transect the uterus between the hemostats and remove the ovaries, horns, and uterine body in one piece. Hold the ends of the caudally placed ligature and remove the remaining hemostat there. If no hemorrhage occurs, let the stump slip back into the pelvis.

Close the peritoneum and muscle with a continuous running suture, taking care that the edges cleanly approximate and that no devitalized tissue is caught in the sutures. The suture should not be pulled so tight that it produces a pouch-string effect. The fragility of the peritoneum in the rabbit makes its handling difficult. Its appearance often simulates very thin fascia.

Close the skin flaps with nonabsorbable, interrupted sutures or a mattress suture.

Because the animal is to be allowed to recover, it is best to inject an antibiotic over the closed cutaneous wound. Wrap a bandage around the abdominal wall to prevent the rabbit from tearing its external sutures. Remember that if the bandage is too tight, venous return and breathing may be affected.

Remove the rabbit to a clean cage, with access to water only. Observe the behavior of the animal for several days postoperatively and evaluate any signs of disease.

The student should read about expected changes in behavior in an animal extensively spayed (castrated) such that the ovaries are included in the excision.

With proper surgical aftercare, these rabbits should have an uneventful recovery.

Exercise 43   **The Physiologic Role of the Placental Anterior Pituitary-like Hormone, Chorionic Gonadotropin**

In pregnancy the placenta secretes large quantities of hormones. One of these is *chorionic gonadotropin*. The concentration of this hormone, which is secreted early in pregnancy by the syncytial trophoblastic cells into the fluids of the mother, can first be measured about 8 days after human female ovulation, just as the fertilized egg is beginning to implant in the uterine endometrium. The rate of secretion rises to a maximum about 7 weeks after ovulation, becoming very low at 16 weeks.

The function of chorionic gonadotropin is to prevent regression of the corpus luteum and to stimulate the corpus luteum to secrete considerable quantities of progesterone and estrogens. The hormones produced are essential to the maintenance of pregnancy.

For many years the question as to whether pregnancy had occurred in the human female was tested by biologic procedures based on demonstrating the effect of human blood or urine containing chorionic gonadotropin upon the ovarian function of an animal. The Freidman test was once commonly used in that regard. It is based upon the production in the pregnant human female of chorionic gonadotropin which is excreted in her urine. When such urine is injected into a nonpregnant rabbit, it produces ovulatory activity in the rabbit, evidenced by ruptured or hemorrhagic follicles.

Biologic tests for pregnancy have all but disappeared as immunologic tests have been developed. The most recent development is in the field of radioimmune assay. The directions herein utilize the classical biologic procedure for pregnancy testing, but the primary goal here is directed toward training the student in surgical technique and increasing his knowledge of the endocrine control of reproduction.

PROCEDURE

Since historic pregnancy testing can be demonstrated as a sideline of the present procedure, isolate the rabbits in individual cages for about 5 weeks prior to use to make sure that they are not pregnant.

Sponge with alcohol the ear of a nonpregnant female rabbit weighing not less than 4 lb and not less than 17 weeks old. Immature rabbits will produce false negative reactions if human pregnancy is being tested for. Make an injection of 15–20 ml of fresh human pregnancy urine into an ear vein. The urine should have been filtered and made lukewarm. Since the hormone is more active in an acid medium, add 10% acetic acid by drops until the human urine is acid to nitrazine paper. For ordinary laboratory purposes, where pregnancy urine is not readily available, commercial preparations of chorionic gonadotropic hormones may be substituted.

Anesthetize the rabbit with sodium pentobarbital 48 hours after the first injection of urine. Do a laparotomy by first cutting through the skin of the ventral abdominal wall, in the midline. Then cut through the muscles and peritoneum at one time, exposing the visceral organs. Locate the ovaries and oviducts by gently pulling the organs out of the abdominal cavity with a blunt tenaculum.

Examine the ovaries for ruptured or hemorrhagic follicles, or for several corpora lutea, which can be seen macroscopically. If a control is desired, examine the ovaries of a rabbit injected with nonpregnant urine; its ovaries should be white or light pink and contain large intact follicles. Positive reactions indicating pregnancy are seen in the rabbit if conception has occurred in 10–14 days in the human from whom the urine was taken.

In closing the abdominal cavity, repair the peritoneum and muscles at one time with chromic catgut. Then approximate the skin edges with nonabsorbable, interrupted sutures.

Observe the rabbit carefully in the postsurgical period so that it may come to full recovery. In the first 24 hours, give water freely, but withhold food.

Review the chemistry, physiologic action, and relationships of chorionic gonadotropin.

Exercise 44   **The Endocrine Function of the Testis;** **Castration**

Use three young male rabbits, one serving as a control. Castrate the second rabbit and keep it for 1 week. Castrate the third rabbit also, but give it 0.1 mg or more of testosterone propionate subcutaneously every day for 1 week. After that time euthanatize all three rabbits, then remove and carefully weigh their seminal vesicles. All the rabbits should be the white New Zealand variety and be approximately the same size and weight.

The seminal vesicles of untreated castrates tend to sharply decrease in size and weight. The seminal vesicles of testosterone-treated castrates tend to maintain their size and weight, and it is not unusual for them to show an increase in these properties.

A. SURGICAL PROCEDURE FOR CASTRATION

1. Sterilize all instruments. Use aseptic technique throughout the procedures.

2. Anesthetize the rabbit with sodium pentobarbital. Shave the hair around the scrotal region. Swab the area with soap and water followed by 70% alcohol.

3. Make a ventral midline incision through the skin of the scrotum. If the testes should spontaneously retract into the abdomen at any time, apply slight pressure over the pelvis to bring them back into the scrotum.

4. Expose the freely movable testes. Draw one testis through the cutaneous incision. Free this testis by cutting through the enveloping tunica.

5. Make a double ligature, that is, two threads tied close to one another, around the spermatic cord. Cut the spermatic cord between the two ligatures. Remove the testis and the attached stump of the spermatic cord.

6. Remove the other testis and the spermatic cord stump in the same way.

7. Close the wound with interrupted sutures, using a small curved needle and fine nonabsorbable sutures.

B. REMOVAL OF THE SEMINAL VESICLES

One week or more after the surgery, euthanatize all the castrated rabbits. Also euthanatize the control rabbits. Locate all structures described below.

Expose the abdominal cavity in the pelvic region. The seminal vesicle lies on the dorsal aspect of the base of the urinary bladder. It is a flattened pouch, about 1 inch long, covered to a great extent by the vesicular and prostate gland. It occupies a median position. Its thin ventral wall is closely adherent to the expanded ends of the deferent ducts. These ducts end in the ventral wall of the seminal vesicle. The tip of the seminal vesicle has a fairly thick muscular wall. The tip is directed forward and is divided slightly to correspond with its inner bilobed cavity. Dissect the urinary bladder down to its stalk. This exposes the full length of the seminal vesicle. Free the seminal vesicle of all structures connected to it.

The urogenital system of the male rabbit is also characterized by other glands. The vesicular and prostate glands are in the dorsal wall of the more posterior aspect of the seminal vesicle, with the vesicular gland being in front of the prostate. The vesicular gland has a pair of ventral ducts that enter the urethra at an oval elevation called the seminal colliculus. The prostate gland has 4–6 tiny ducts on either side of the colliculus.

There is a variable number of paraprostic glands that are projections of the urethra at either side of the base of the seminal vesicle.

Cowper's (bulbourethral) gland is a bilobed structure located behind the prostate in the dorsolateral walls of the urethra.

Dissect the seminal vesicles down to the stalk and remove them. Lay them between two pieces of moistened filter paper in a covered Petri dish. Weigh the seminal vesicles in mg from all of the rabbits and compare all results. A sample protocol is given below:

1. Control, not castrated, noninjected   950
2. Castrate, noninjected   275
3. Castrate, injected with testosterone   670

For a description of the urogenital organs of the rabbit, along with a bibliography of sources for the embryonic and adult morphology, consult Elchlepp, (1952).

Exercise 1 **Chronic Intravenous Catheterization**

Chronic cannulation of vessels is desirable if frequent blood collections are necessary and the ear veins become a progressively inaccessible source. Hall *et al.* (1974) described a useful method of chronic cannulation which the present writers recommend.

Use Medical-Grade Silastic tubing (Dow Corning Corp., Medical Products Div., Midland, Michigan), 0.04 inches I.D. and 0.085 inches O.D. Wash about 30 cm of the tubing in detergent solution, rinse it thoroughly in distilled water, autoclave it at 15 lb pressure for 15 minutes, and store it if desired. If stored, rinse the tubing before use in sterile water and then in sterile 0.9% sodium chloride solution. Before implantation, fill the tubing with saline containing 1500 units of heparin. In a later phase of the procedure, as directed herein, place a 3-way Tomac stopcock (American Hospital Supply Corp., Evanston, Illinois), to which is attached an 18-gauge needle, in the upper, free terminal end of the tubing.

Lightly anesthetize a rabbit through an ear vein with sodium pentobarbital. Clip the fur, and shave the skin of the ventral and lateral neck and also of the interscapular area. Paint these cutaneous areas with 2% iodine. Infiltrate the sites to be incised (below) with 1% lidocaine (Xylocaine hydrochloride) to suppress any incisional pain.

Make a 4-cm median ventral neck incision extending caudally from the level of the hyoid bone toward the sternal manubrium. Expose the right external jugular vein by dividing the overlying muscle.

Follow the jugular vein upward until it bifurcates to the anterior (ventral) and posterior (dorsal) facial veins. Starting just above the origin of the posterior facial vein, clear away connective tissue from about 2 cm of that vessel. Apply a bulldog clamp to the posterior facial vein at the bifurcation. Using No. 4–0 suture, ligate the vein, above the clamp. Keep the suture ends long. Place a second ligature below the bulldog clamp, but do not tie it.

Make a small incision in the vein, cranial to the clamp, but caudal to the more cephalic ligature and insert the catheter. Remove the bulldog clamp and gently push the catheter caudally to reach the right cranial vena cava. Tighten the caudal ligature to secure the catheter at that point. Then secure the catheter at the more cranial region where it was inserted, with the long ends of the cephalic ligature. Seal the cephalic (terminal) end of the catheter by folding the end over and tying twice with suture, leaving the ends long.

It is then necessary to protect and also to have access to the catheter which is to be imbedded in a skin-fold tunnel on the dorsal neck.

Make a pouch, 4 cm in diameter, subcutaneously on the right side of the neck, beginning at the place of the prior median ventral cutaneous incision. Grip the sutures on the tied end of the catheter with a hemostat. Direct the hemostat dorsally in the subcutaneous space towards the center of the neck dorsal to the spine. Make a small incision and exteriorize the sutures and catheter through the opening. A loop of catheter is formed in the subcutaneous pocket in the lateral aspect of the neck. The loop buffers the stress on the catheter during neck movements.

Close the original midventral neck skin incision with skin clips or sutures. In the lateral neck, tie two ligatures 1 cm apart and 1 cm behind the terminal loop. These should secure the catheter without hindering blood flow. Position the catheter in the midline with the end loop pointing caudally. Use the loose ends of the ligatures to suture the skin over the catheter, thus forming a protective tunnel. Use a third suture distal to the previous one. Do not tie it. It provides an invagination to hide the looped end of the catheter.

In use, withdraw the terminal loop in the catheter from its pocket, untie it, and insert on it an 18-gauge needle with a 3-way stopcock. Draw the heparinized saline out through one sidearm and discard it. Draw a desired blood sample from the other sidearm. Refill the system with heparinized saline. Reform the terminal loop, tie it off and replace it in the pouch. To prevent clotting in the catheter over a period of several weeks, renew the heparinized saline periodically.

Exercise 2   Surgical External Biliary Fistula

A procedure is described for preparing a biliary fistula which involves the insertion of a catheter into the distal end of the gallbladder. The method was devised by Boegli and Hall (1969).

Anesthetize a fasted rabbit with sodium pentobarbital by ear-vein injection and prepare the animal for a right lateral abdominal incision. Position the rabbit in a modified left lateral recumbency such that the hind legs are secured in a supine position. After draping, make a 7-cm right lateral rectus incision parallel to the superior mammary vein. Free the fascia and fat of the ventrally exposed liver lobes by blunt dissection. Free the gallbladder from the liver. Incise the distal end of the gallbladder, partially drain it, and insert a 2.0 mm O.D. catheter to about 2 mm from the gallbladder neck. Secure the catheter by double ligation of the free end of the gallbladder which contains the catheter.

Use blunt dissection to expose the common bile duct. The duct is covered with fat and is usually not clearly defined. Take care in dissecting since the vena cava is attached to the same fascia as that covering the common duct. Pass a blunt-ended hemostat beneath the common duct. Pull a silk ligature under the duct with the hemostat and ligate the duct. Avoid ligation of the pancreatic duct or the vena cava. Remove all sponges and instruments and cover the area with warm, saline-moistened, surgical sponges. The duct can be considered patent if 16–20 cm of bile rises in the catheter in 15 minutes. Close the wound by standard suturing procedure.

Bring the catheter up to the dorsal surface and apply a dressing. Wrap cotton around the body trunk in the area of the incision. Cover this with wide gauze and then apply tape. Take care to keep the dressing loose so that breathing is not inhibited. Externalize the catheter tip through the dressing. Attach a 125-ml polyethylene wash bottle to the dressing on the side opposite the incision. Shorten the wash bottle delivery tube and attach the catheter for bile collection. Drill a small hole in the bottle top to equalize pressure.

Use standard postsurgical care. The administration of subcutaneous fluids and nutritives is useful. Boegli and Hall (1969) used an oral bile salt substitute in place of drinking water to aid in animal survival. This substitute consisted of sodium, potassium, calcium, and magnesium salts. Properly maintained rabbits should live for 5–8 days and yield 200 to 500 ml of bile.

Exercise 3 Cerebral Ventricle Perfusion of the Conscious Rabbit

Moir and Dow (1970) developed a method for perfusing the cerebral ventricles in the conscious rabbit. In their procedure, guide tubes directed toward the ventricles plus a curved guide directed toward the cisterna magna are implanted in the rabbit skull. This method is about 75% effective in tapping cerebrospinal fluid by percutaneous puncture, using the guide tubes. The procedure also allows ventriculocisternal perfusion in the conscious animal. Moir and Dow stated that cerebrospinal fluid is formed at a mean rate of 0.006 ml/min in the rabbit.

Select mature male rabbits, preferably 3.5 kg, and administer general anesthesia. Infiltrate the subcutaneous tissues of the scalp and the back of the neck with a local anesthetic. Surgically prepare the neck and scalp, and continue with sterile operating technique.

Make a midline incision and reflect laterally for 1 cm the temporal muscles over the skull. Support the head so that the lambda is in a plane 1 mm below the bregma. Hold the skull template (Fig. 33) in position and mark the points for drilling the lateral ventricle guide tube holes. Drill holes through these points with a 2-mm drill and securely screw the guide tubes into place (Fig. 34A). The guide tubes are properly positioned when they point toward the bodies of the ventricles, but are about 2 mm above their lumina. This prevents leakage of cerebrospinal fluid and distortion of the ventricles.

Check the correct location of the guide tubes by using a 25-gauge needle attached to a silicone rubber tube filled with a column of artificial cerebrospinal fluid and retained with a small clamp. The fluid column should be 15 cm high with a diameter of 0.16 mm. Insert the needle into the guide tube and advance it 1 mm past the tip of the guide tube. Release the clamp and slowly advance the needle. When the needle

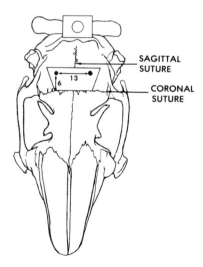

Figure 33.   Skull template in position on skull.

Figure 34.   Guide tubes. (A) For ventricles; (B) for cisterna magna.

enters the lateral ventricle, a slow fall should occur in the CSF column.

Flex the rabbit's head and extend the midline incision caudally. Incise the nuchal ligament longitudinally and retract the posterior neck muscles laterally to permit visualization of the occipital bone and the atlantooccipital membrane. Reflect laterally the muscles over the superior surface of the occipital protuberance and drill a 0.7-mm hole in the midline. Drill the hole starting from the small recess in the occipital bone just rostral to the occipital protuberance. The hole in passing through the protuberance is to be continued in the midline toward the atlantooccipital membrane as a groove in the dorsal aspect of the occipital bone.

Choose an appropriately long, curved guide tube (Fig. 34B) and push it into the hole such that the opening at the tip of the tube is in close approximation to the edge of the atlantooccipital membrane. The curve at the tip lets the needle approach the cisterna magna from an optimal direction. Place a small, stainless-steel screw In the occipital bone close to the guide tube and then surround both with acrylic dental cement. When the cement has hardened, approximate the nuchal muscles and close the skin.

Rabbits can be used for perfusion studies about 2 weeks postoperatively. In doing this, immobilize a rabbit in a restraint box. Insert a 25 = /gauge, 3.2-cm long needle into the cisterna magna guide tube with the tip opening facing rostrally. Advance the needle by gentle tapping. Puncture is completed when there is a flow of CSF.

Exercise 4   **Gastrotomy**

A gastrotomy is a surgical entrance into the stomach. This is performed on animals to remove foreign bodies such as hair balls and to relieve pressure from gastric distention. Gastrotomies may be performed to sample gastric contents, and to place experimental compounds directly into the stomach when the use of stomach tubes is not desirable. A gastrotomy is also a procedure to remove specific portions of the stomach wall.

Anesthetize the rabbit and secure it firmly to the surgical table, in the position of dorsal recumbancy. Prepare it for sterile, midline, ventral abdominal surgery.

With a midline incision expose the stomach. Carefully pack off the stomach with gauze sponges. The stomach should be completely isolated from other abdominal organs to prevent general contamination when the stomach is opened and its nonsterile contents are exposed.

If possible, the stomach incision should be made in a visibly bloodless area perpendicular to the greater curvature. If research reasons dictate that another area be used, maximum hemostasis must be maintained. Use a scalpel to incise down to the mucosal lining and then a scissors to complete the entry. Discard the scissors from the sterile instruments because of contamination from the gastric contents. The surgeon may prefer to place a simple inverted suture (Lembert) at each end of the proposed suture line and use the long ends of the suture for stomach wall immobilization while proceeding with the surgical manipulation. After the stomach is entered, complete the desired procedure. The team must be fully aware that it is dealing with surgical contaminants after the gastric mucosa is incised.

Close the gastric incision with No. 000 chromic surgical gut, a straight taper needle, and an inverting suture pattern such as the Lembert. Close the abdominal cavity in the routine manner.

Aftercare consists of a soft or liquid diet for 3 days, and supportive fluid therapy if indicated. It is advisable to administer postsurgical antibiotics since entry was made into the gastrointestinal tract and there is a great potential for peritonitis to occur.

Exercise 5   Cystotomy

Cystotomy, or surgical entrance into the urinary bladder, is performed to remove calculi, to help remove masses, and for exploratory purposes. Cystotomies in investigation are done for the direct sampling of bladder wall tissues and for the implantation of experimental materials. Thus, zinc pellets or other materials may be implanted to serve as nuclei for stone formation.

Anesthetize a rabbit, place it in dorsal recumbency, and prepare it for sterile surgery. Make a ventral, midline incision starting from the umbilicus and running caudally in the pelvic region. Expose the pelvic visceral organs.

Elevate the urinary bladder and isolate it as much as possible from other pelvic organs by packing the bladder with sterile gauze sponges. This should prevent possible later contamination of peritoneal contents by any urine that may be expressed through the opened bladder.

Incise the bladder over a relatively avascular area of the fundus. Stay or holding sutures may be helpful to immobilize or aid in bladder manipulations. Then carry out the desired procedure.

1. *Calculi removal.* Remove any calculi with forceps and irrigate the bladder with warm isotonic saline solution to wash out small particles. Pass a urethral catheter caudally to flush out particles that may have accumulated in the urethra.

2. *Neoplasia removal.* Isolate and remove any mass with special attention being given to control hemorrhage.

3. *Foreign implants.* Use stay sutures to elevate the bladder. Then make a small stab wound with a pointed scalpel. With forceps, insert the foreign material into the bladder. (*Note:* Place liquid materials into the bladder of a male rabbit by catheterization.)

Close the bladder with No. 000 chromic gut, using an inverting suture pattern. If the bladder wall is extremely thickened because of cystitis, it may be advisable to butt the edges by suturing the mucosa and part of the muscularis and to apply a second row of interrupted sutures in the serosa and in a superficial portion of the muscularis.

Remove the packing and close the abdominal wall. Clinically monitor the rabbit for several days. Do urinalysis and culturing if it appears necessary.

Exercise 6 **Aseptic Bone Marrow Aspiration**

Place a rabbit on the surgery table and anesthetize it. Shave and prepare the lateral surface of the animal's thigh for sterile surgery. Position the rabbit with the prepared leg tied in a tightly flexed posture, then drape the surgical site.

Using sterile technique, make a 10-cm incision in the femur area in the depression between the vastus intermedius and biceps femoris muscles. Clip sterile gauze sponges to the edges of the skin and evert the gauze to prevent skin contamination of the operative field. Do blunt dissection through the fascia and muscles to expose the femur. Retract the muscles and scrape the exposed femoral shaft with a curette. Then swab the bone with tincture of iodine.

Drill two holes in the femur 4–5 cm apart. Seat two hypodermic needles that have been reground to short bevels and dull points in the holes, with the bevels facing each other. The drill size and needle gauge must be matched to provide a firm fit; for example, a 1/16 in drill (0.159 cm) and a 16-gauge needle will allow an acceptable fit.

Attach a syringe containing 5–7 ml of a balanced salt solution to one needle and attach an empty syringe to a second needle. Apply gentle digital pressure to the plunger of the filled syringe. Aspirate the empty syringe which collects the bone marrow sample. Repeat washings are generally not required. After marrow collection, remove the needles and close the wound.

If it is desired to determine the amount of peripheral blood in the marrow sample, use the Evans blue dye injection technique described by Powsner and Fly (1962).

Exercise 7   **The Regional Removal of the Uterine Endometrium**

David *et al.* (1974) described a technique followed herein for excising the full thickness of the endometrium in a well-defined area under direct vision. Female white rabbits were used, confined in individual cages for 18–21 days to avoid a pseudopregnant hormonal state and to maintain uniform conditions of estrus.

Following stabilization as described above, anesthetize a rabbit by injection or inhalant anesthesia. Perform a laparotomy under sterile conditions. Inspect the uterus and adnexa to exclude visible pathologic changes.

Make a 4.5–5.0 cm longitudinal excision on the antimesometrial side or wall of each horn, exposing the endometrium. Excise the endometrium under direct vision, using small, straight scissors. Cautiously raise the endometrium with forceps and excise a desired section of it depthwise down to the muscular layer. Remove any residual endometrial patches. Some investigators might want to limit the denuded area to about 4 x 1 cm.

Close the uterine incision with a continuous suture, using No. 3–0 catgut. Then close the body wall. At the termination of the operative procedure, inject intramuscularly 150,000 I.U. of crystalline sodium penicillin G.

REGENERATION

If it is desired to study regeneration of the endometrium, compare the operated horn with the other horn. To do this, perform laparotomies on a series of previously operated rabbits, starting 24 hours following excision of the endometrium and at daily intervals for 14 days thereafter. Remove both uterine horns, fix and dehydrate parts of the material, embed the tissues in paraffin, section them, and stain the sections with hematoxylin and eosin, or with other stains.

David *et al.* (1974) found that endometrial regeneration appeared only after 24 hours, originating from the surface epithelium of the intact areas. The denuded area was completely covered in 3 days.

Exercise 8   Fetal Derivation by Hysterotomy and Hysterectomy

Cesarean delivery, or "aseptic derivation," may be required for embryological studies, for establishing germ-free rabbit colonies, and for the management of fetal or maternal dystocia. The anesthetic adminstered to the doe may vary with experimental requirements and with the preference of the investigator. Ether or methoxyflurane administered to achieve a light plane of anesthesia and then supplemented with an epidural block or local infiltration with Xylocaine is satisfactory. The animal can then be placed in dorsal recumbency and prepared for sterile surgery.

Make a midline incision in the ventral abdominal wall passing through the skin and linea alba. The incision is to extend from the xiphoid cartilage to the brim of the pubis. Avoid mammary tissue that may be engorged in preparation for lactation of the neonate. With this in mind, some surgeons prefer to make a lateral flank approach for exposure of the uterus. Proceed with alternatives as follows.

A. HYSTEROTOMY

Locate the uterus. Exteriorize both horns and rotate them so that the dorsal surface of the uterus is uppermost. Make an incision in the midline of the dorsal surface of the uterine body. Pull the first pup (kindling) through the incision. If the placental sac is intact, tear or cut the sac and strip it from the pup. Place two hemostats on the umbilical cord 1 cm from the pup's body. Cut the cord between the hemostats and give the pup with a hemostat to an assistant. Use the second hemostat to gently pull the placenta away from its maternal attachments. In a milkinglike maneuver, bring any other pups to the uterine incision and remove each in the manner described.

Close the uterine incision with a continuous row of inverting Lembert or Cushing sutures. Use chromic No. 00 surgical gut. Close the abdominal wall and skin in the routine manner.

B. HYSTERECTOMY

Locate the uterus and exteriorize it. Apply crushing-type forceps (Carmelts) to the cranial end of each horn. Apply another (third) forceps caudal to the uterine body but cranial to the cervix. Cut the uterus so that it is free from all attachments. Remove it with the three forceps still attached. Research procedures usually do not require that the doe be saved and it could be euthanatized at this point. If survival of the doe is required, hemostasis must be provided before the uterus is removed.

Pass the closed uterus containing the pups through germicidical traps into Trexler isolators or manipulate otherwise as may be required. In the next step, remove the pups from the uterus, strip the placental membranes from the pups, and clamp the umbilical cords as previously described.

C. NEWBORN CARE

The assistant who receives a newborn pup should first check to see that the placental membranes have been removed and then he should proceed with clearing of the pup's airways. Use gauze sponges to clear mucus and debris from the mouth and nostrils. Open the mouth of the pup, then swab and dry the mouth to prevent inhalation pneumonia and to aid in the stimulation of respiration. Rub the pup vigorously while drying it. This stimulates respiration and circulation. If the pup does not display a pink color and it is not breathing rhythmically at this point, hold it firmly in a towel and swing it with its head down, using a centrifugal arc motion to remove fluid from its lungs.

Remove the hemostat on the umbilicus and observe the umbilical stump to see that it is totally occluded. Apply a swab wetted with tincture of iodine to the umbilical cord to prevent subsequent infection if the animal is not in a sterile environment.

Exercise 9   **Artificial Vagina for Collection of Semen**

The rabbit is a valid model for the study of reproductive physiology. If, for example, semen samples from rabbit males are being studied, there must be adequate methods for collection of semen and this can be accomplished by the use of an artificial vagina (A.V.). The first A.V. was designed in 1914 for the dog, but since that time various types have come into use which are suitable for other mammals, e.g., bull, ram, horse, boar.

The apparatus for the rabbit has evolved from a glass receptacle covered by rabbit pelt to simulate the vagina to rubber hose pipe and then to latex liners. A satisfactory polyethylene tube containing a latex liner was described by Walton (1958). Bredderman *et al.* (1964) described a modification.

Hollow out a 2-inch diameter polyethylene rod to a tube and line it with a latex liner. Figure 35 illustrates the construction.

Fill the space between the walls of the tube and the internal liner with water at about 45°C. The temperature, which can be recorded periodically by inserting a thermometer into the A.V., is maintained fairly uniformly since polyethylene is a good insulator. The temperature is higher than that of the rabbit's body (38°–40°C), but this compensates for a small temperature differential due to some insulation of the rubber lining and of a petroleum jelly layer which will separate the penis to be inserted into the liner from the surrounding water compartment. The heat is needed to stimulate heat-sensitive nerve endings on the surface of the penis. The petroleum jelly is lightly applied with a glass rod to the inner aspect of the sheath prior to penetration by the male rabbit.

The pressure in the A.V. must not be great enough to provide resistance to entry of the rabbit's penis. Test this by inserting the small finger, lubricated with petroleum jelly, into the A.V. If the pressure is correct, the finger enters easily. The larger index finger should meet some resistance. It is also necessary to ascertain, by trial and error, the appropriate angle at which the A.V. is presented to the male.

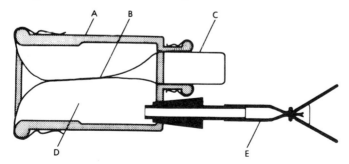

Figure 35. Artificial vagina. (A) Wall of hollow polyethylene rod; (B) latex liner; (C) area for collection and storage of sample; (D) space for warm water; and (E) insert tube for thermometer.

In presenting the A.V., hold the device, with its opening pointing toward the male, between the hind legs of the doe. When the buck mounts, its penis enters the open lubricated end of the A.V. and the ejaculate is collected therein. When a buck is trained to use the A.V., the doe need no longer be used. Instead, the operator can wear a glove covered with rabbit skin, worn fur outwards on his hand that holds the A.V.

Following use, rinse the latex liner with water, dust it with powder, wash off the powder, and dry the sheath with an air jet.

Exercise 10   **Transfer of Rabbit Ova**

Procedures have been developed in many mammalian species for surgical recovery of fertilized ova from the uterus and for their transfer to the uteri of recipient mammals. For details of the procedure that was originally adapted to rabbits, the reader is referred to Hafez (1961).

If recovered fertilized ova which are transferred are to develop successfully, the developmental stages of the eggs transferred must closely approximate the developmental uterine stage of the recipient female. Survival is best with eggs of the same age as, or one day older than, the stage of uterine development. If the fertilized eggs are stored at low temperature, this may overcome the asynchronism of ovulation in donors and recipient females. Cooling should be slow to prevent "temperature shock." Storage of 2-blastomere rabbit ova at $0°C$ permits survival for 96–120 hours (Hafez, 1961).

For manipulation of the ova while storing them *in vitro* for transfer, various liquid media are available. Such media usually include blood serum as an ingredient (e.g., Ringer-Locke solution plus an equal volume of homologous blood serum). In using heterlogous serum, avoid that of man, sheep, cattle, goat, or fowl since these contain ovicidal factors against rabbit ova.

A storage period may remove ovicidal factors in certain heterologous blood. In this procedure, incubate the blood at $37°C$ for 30 minutes, centrifuge the blood twice, and then store the serum in a refrigerator for one or two days prior to transplantation.

The heterologous sera of horse, dog, guinea pig, rat, and pig do not appear to carry ovicidal factors for the rabbit egg. In obtaining their sera as a medium for the ova, obtain cardiac blood from a donor under sterile conditions one or two hours prior to euthanatizing the donor. Let the blood coagulate in an autoclaved centrifuge tube and then centrifuge the blood at 3000 rpm.

It is possible to transfer ova directly without storage. If stored, the present writers concur in the recommendation of Hafez in advising storage in 7% gelatin media (i.e., autoclaved gel of pure gelatin, U.S.P., dissolved in a 1 to 1 serum–0.9% sodium chloride solution). Hafez found that after storing fertilized ova in this gelatin medium for 4 hours, the degree of successful implantation of the morulae was 72%. After 144 hours, it declined to 31%. These values were higher than those found for ova stored only in liquid serum media for corresponding times.

Use conditioned, prepubertal or adult does. If it is to be prepubertal does which will serve as donors of ova, superovulate these does with gonadotropic hormones. Hafez' schedule was as follows: he injected the donors subcutaneously with 50 I.U. Equimex pregnant mare serum (Ayerst), again at the same time the second day, then 28 hours later the third day. On the fourth day, 22 hours after the third injection, he administered intravenously 2 I.U. of the gonadotropin called Vetrophin (Abbott) or else 50 I.U. of Gonadogen (Upjohn). Because of the obsolescence of some of the trademarked names, use pregnant mare serum purchased under its generic name.

Kennelly and Foote (1965) compared the superovulatory effect of several commercially available gonadotropins. Superovulation was consistently achieved in Dutch-belted rabbits, at least 16 weeks of age, injected subcutaneously twice daily for 3 days with follicle-stimulating hormone (FSH Armour) dissolved in 0.9% saline. At 16 weeks, a total of 0.31 mg FSH/day produced marked ovulatory response. In the adults (over 20 weeks), 0.50 mg FSH/day was effective. Age should be the principal criterion when selecting female rabbits for gonadotropic treatment leading to superovulation.

Glass (1972) used 50 I.U. of human chorionic gonadotropin (APL, Ayerst) for inducing superovulation in New Zealand white rabbits.

Shortly after injection, when ovulation is expected, mate the prospective female donors to known fertile bucks. In 18 to 48 hours postcoitum, euthanatize the donors (by bleeding, preferably).

To recover the fertilized ova, in their developmental stages in the donor, perform a laparotomy, expose the Fallopian tubes, remove the eggs and place them in sterile Petri dishes. To obtain the ova, flush the tubes with a few milliliters of sterilized 0.9% saline solution. Use a syringe and a blunt 22-gauge needle secured in the infundibular end with a ligature.

Observe the presence of ova under a stereoscopic binocular microscope. They may be counted, if desired, at a magnification of 35 ×. Select morphologically normal ova for transfer.

There should be available at the time of transfer synchronous pseudopregnant recipients. To induce a pseudopregnancy which is synchronous with the stage of development of the stored ova, mate the recipient female rabbits to vasectomized bucks.

At 8 days postcoitum anesthetize the preudopregnant recipients with sodium pentobarbital. Perform a laparotomy on both flanks. Transfer 3–8 fertilized ova of the donor into each Fallopian tube of the recipient. Puncture the tubes with a micropipette that contains the fertilized eggs. Spray 25,000 I.U./ml of penicillin into the abdomen near the incision. Close the abdomen with chromic gut (Ethicon).

If laparotomized at 8 days postcoitum, necropsy the recipients later (e.g., 15 days) if determinations of embryonic development of the eggs are to be made.

Transplantation of eggs can be useful in genetic and physiologic studies. It can help to determine whether the egg or the tube is at fault in faulty pregnancies. It suggests the influence of the uterine environment upon the developing embryo.

Exercise 11   Sexing Newborn Rabbits

Sawin *et al.* (1938) described a procedure to sex newborn rabbits. Hatez (1970) stated that sexing is much more determinate if performed not earlier than 3 weeks after birth. Fox and Crary (1972) slightly modified Sawin's procedure and it is their procedure that the present writers find acceptable and which is presented herein.

For external sexing hold the newborn animal facing you. Palpate the genital orifice and exert mild pressure on either side of the urogenital papilla. Place the thumb and forefinger as close as possible to the penis or vulva to avoid using undue pressure.

The penis is felt as a rounded mass, protruding evenly on all sides. The vulva protrudes only ventrally. The anus-to-vulva distance is greater than the anus-to-penis distance.

The reader is referred to Fox and Crary (1972) for sexing prematurely born rabbits, as early as 23 days of gestation, by internal examination involving dissection and magnification of the gonadal structures.

Exercise 12   Identification of Rabbits by Tattooing

Rabbit identification by tattoo is a standard procedure. The present writers recommend a procedure with a commercial tattoo machine (such as Model 400 Tattoo Machine, Ancare Corp., Manhasset, New York) whose use was described in detail by Castor and Zaldivar (1973). The principle of operation is standard. A needle vibrated by electric current deposits particulate pigment into the skin.

Tattooing of the rabbit's ear without prior local anesthesia is a stressful action and the rabbit thereafter resists attempts at bloodletting and is generally more difficult to manage. To reduce local pain during tatooing, a nerve block should be performed. This is accomplished by two sub-cutaneous injections of 2% procaine, with or without supplementary epinephrine. This can effectively anesthetize two branches of the external auditory nerve which innervate the area to be tattooed, i.e., the inner surface of an ear between the midline and the lower edge of the ear. Locate the external auditory nerve in the midline of the dorsal surface of the ear. The nerve, median artery, and vein travel together. Inject 0.2 ml of the procaine solution close to those blood vessels near the base of the ear, taking care not to pierce the vessels.

Inject another 0.2 ml close to the marginal vein where it passes, accompanied by the auricular branch of the facial nerve, along the lower margin of the inner surface of the ear. Warm the ear prior to each injection to increase the effectiveness of the anesthetic.

Tattoo the ear between 5 and 15 minutes following the second injection of the anesthetic. The tattooing is done by applying a layer of India ink or other tattoo ink to the ear surface. The desired numbers are then slowly outlined using the tip of the tattoo instrument like a pencil. The ink is then again spread over the tattooed area. Excessive ink is wiped off. The tattoo will be clearly defined in about three days after the remaining ink on the ear has dissipated itself. The tattoo remains permanently visible in the ear. Do not use the needle close to the tip of the ear since the prior injections anesthetize two, but not the third branch of the nerve. The third branch supplies half of the ear contralateral to the tattoo area and also parts of the tip of the ear.

Exercise 13 Pyrogen Testing in Rabbits

It is necessary to determine that pharmaceutical products are non-pyrogenic, i.e., do not contain fever-producing agents. There are two official pyrogen tests: (1) the United States Pharmacopeia Test (U.S. Pharmacopeia, 1970) for nonbiologic products, and (2) the Public Health Service Regulations (U.S. National Institutes of Health, 1969). The test solution is injected intravenously into rabbits and rectal temperatures are recorded. The procedures have been reviewed for rabbits by Weary and Wallin (1973).

Select healthy New Zealand rabbits, 2.0–2.5 kg body weight, preferably females because of greater ease in handling. Keep them at uniform room temperature. Feed them commercial rabbit pellets, and water freely. During the test withhold food only, starting 24 hours prior to testing. Select rabbits for test only if their initial body temperatures are between 38.9° and 39.8°C (and not higher). Determine their body temperature with a clinical thermometer lubricated with petroleum jelly and inserted rectally to a depth of at least 7.5 cm and held therein for 2 minutes. If considerable numbers of rabbits are to be tested, use electric thermometers having copper–constantan thermocouples or thermistors and connect the outputs to chart recorders. Restrain the rabbits in boxes to allow the rectal probes to remain in place throughout the test.

Cage each rabbit separately. Weigh each before use to calculate the required dose of test substance to be injected. Insert the lubricated probes or rectal thermometers. Stabilize the rabbits in a state of undisturbed rest for 30 minutes prior to recording their baseline control temperatures. Administer the test substance within 40 minutes of taking the control temperature.

For injection, dry heat the syringes, needles, and glassware at 250°C for 30 minutes. Autoclaving does not ensure that these items are pyrogen-free.

Slowly inject the test solutions, which have been warmed to 37°C, into an ear vein at a dose of 10 ml/kg body weight. The needles can vary from 20-gauge × 1 inch to 22-gauge × 1 inch, depending upon the volumes to be injected. Dilate the vein by suspending a 15-watt lighted bulb just above the ear. Note the time when the injection is terminated. Record rectal temperatures 1, 2, and 3 hours thereafter.

The U.S.P. test states that the result is presumptively positive if one of three rabbits has a temperature increase of 0.6°C above its baseline value, or if the total of the three rabbit temperature rises exceeds 1.4°C. If either result occurs, repeat the test on five other rabbits. Pyrogens are absent if not more than three of the eight rabbits show individual rises of 0.6°C or more, and if the sum of the eight rises does not exceed 3.7°C.

The Public Health Service regulations state that a substance does not meet pyrogen test requirements if half of four or more test rabbits have rises of 0.6°C or more, or if the average rise is 0.5°C or more.

According to the U.S.P., a sham test is also necessary if rabbits are to be put on a pyrogen test for the first time. No intravenous injection is given, but the temperature-recording schedule simulates that of test animals. It is also possible to sham test with pyrogen-free saline solution (Martin and Marcus, 1964). Even in reusing rabbits, perform at least two sham tests. Rest the rabbits given test solutions for 2 weeks before using them again. Do not use the same rabbit more than three times, as a precautionary measure.

PYROGENS

There are a number of pyrogens, primarily of a polysaccharide nature, produced by bacteria, molds, viruses, and yeast. They are common in unsterilized, distilled water. Parenteral drugs can thus be readily contaminated with pyrogens during their preparation. Endotoxins, for example, which are contained in the cell walls of gram-negative bacteria, can rapidly exhibit pyrogenic effects upon injection.

Exercise 14   **Diagnostic Skin Testing in Rabbits**

Skin tests can provide a reliable and sensitive method for detecting certain diseases in rabbits. As an example of their usefulness, Pakes *et al.* (1972) used skin testing to detect rabbit encephalitozoonosis caused by *Encephalitozoon cuniculi*. This disease was not found to be detectable by other known means, thus making identification of noninfected stock for use in research very difficult.

The antigens for inducing reaction in the skin test can be prepared by specific procedures described elsewhere in the appropriate literature. Pakes *et al.* (1972) described the details of their preparation for *E. cuniculi* and the reader is referred to his paper. To test the possibility that reactions may be due to nonspecific stimuli, rabbits should also be skin tested with controls, e.g., diluents or preparations of unifected (tissue culture) cells prepared in the same manner as was the test antigen.

In testing, remove the hair from the abdomen of a rabbit with an animal clipper containing a No. 40 surgical head. Inject intradermally at separate sites on the abdomen 0.1 ml of test antigen and 0.1 ml of control substance in solution. Use a 27-gauge, one-half–inch needle attached to a tuberculin syringe. Circle the injection sites with waterproof ink to facilitate visualization of the responses

Examine the injection sites about 4 hours later and then daily for 5–7 days. Record the diameter and thickness of the reactions in millimeters. Criteria for a positive reaction are areas of induration and erythema several millimeters in diameter and about 1 mm in thickness, at 24–72 hours postinjection. The reactions tend to increase in intensity through the second and third day, depending upon the pathogen-host sensitivity. The color of a positive reaction is pink to dark red.

If histological preparations have been made, a positive skin reaction is typified by infiltration of blood and tissue cells. Lymphocytes, macrophages, and plasma cells may be abundant. Look for these cells especially in the dermis, around blood vessels, and in adnexal structures. In severe reactions there may be necrosis of the inflammatory cells. Edema becomes evident.

The intensity of positive reactions is not necessarily correlated with the severity or distribution of lesions. In negative tests, the responses can vary from no detectable reactions to light pink or orange indurations which are of very small diameter and thickness.

Exercise 15   Collection and Analysis of Peritoneal Fluid

Peritoneal fluid is useful in studies such as inflammation, pregnancy, estrous and menstrual cycles, and cancer. The reader is referred to Davis *et al.* (1974) for a quantitative analysis of the cellular contents of peritoneal fluid in New Zealand white rabbits and for a brief review of the literature about this fluid.

Using firm, but gentle, manual restraint in the unanesthetized rabbit, penetrate the ventral abdominal wall with an 18-gauge needle attached to a 2.5-ml syringe. Use caution not to injure visceral organs.

Gently aspirate the peritoneal fluid. Place aliquots of the fluid onto albumin-coated, clean glass slides. Immerse the slides in 95% ethanol for at least 2 hours.

Stain the slides by the method described by Papanicolaou (1932). Consult his text for identification and description of cellular elements commonly occurring in body fluids.

Identify the cells of the rabbit's peritoneal fluid, grouping them as granulocytes, lymphocytes, monocytes, mast cells, histiocytes, bare nuclei and mesothelial cells.

In counting, select 200 consecutive cells randomly and classify them in the groupings above. It is more practicable to use random counting of a given number of cells than to count the number in a fixed volume, because sometimes only a few drops of fluid can be obtained.

Davis *et al.* (1974) reported that species and sex differences influence the cytologic count of cells, and also that the cellular content of the adult female white rabbit is somewhat similar to that of the human female.

Exercise 16   **Abdominal Paracentesis**

Abdominal paracentesis is a useful procedure for administration of fluids or for withdrawal of fluid for diagnostic, therapeutic, and research purposes.

Anesthetize a rabbit lightly or else heavily sedate it, then place it in lateral recumbency. It is possible to use manual restraint without resorting to analgesic drugs only if the rabbit does not show signs of pain at any stage of the manipulative procedure.

Prepare for sterile surgery an area of about 1 cm^2 in the upper aspect of the ventral abdominal midline, i.e., shave and sterilize the skin. Make a small incision through the skin with a scalpel and then firmly and slowly push a sterile, Kolb abdominal trocar through the abdominal wall just lateral to the linea alba. Partially withdraw the trocar which is within a cannula to clear the openings in the ends of the cannula. Attach a syringe with a three-way stopcock to the cannula for fluid aspiration, injection or abdominal washings.

In some rabbits it may be necessary to use Xylocaine infiltration to alleviate pain in the area of trocar penetration. When inserting the trocar, firm, slow pressure will minimize the possibility of penetrating an abdominal organ. The injection into the abdominal cavity should be far enough forward to prevent penetration into the urinary bladder. Manual expression of urine from the bladder is also useful and should be done before the trocar is passed.

Exercise 17   **Cardiac Monitor for Anesthetized Rabbits**

Banta *et al.* (1972) designed an electronic cardiac auscultation monitor to assist in the objective sensing of cardiopulmonary responses in rabbits which are under general anesthesia. Although the concept has long been established, this particular system is recommended and emphasized herein. The circuit diagram and list of parts for the construction of the monitor are derived from the original paper.

Apply a carbon microphone by an elastic band to the rabbit's thorax. Feed the output of the microphone to a preamplifier, having a filtered circuit and a frequency response of 20 to 100 kilohertz, which allow it to be tuned to the heart sounds (Fig. 36).

Banta considered the preamplifier to be unique. As seen in figure, the base of Q_1 (B_1) and the emitter of Q_2 (E_2) are grounded. This establishes a bias in the gain control (R_5). Additionally, Q_1 and Q_2 are joined ahead of the parallel circuit of C_4 and R_5. This prevents AC currents from disrupting the operating bias. C_1 and C_2 (plus R_4) filter out high frequency sounds before they are effectively amplified and also the high harmonics of the true heart sounds.

The amplifier by way of its 21-V terminal drives the microphone and preamplifier. The effective frequency response of the 4-inch suspension speaker is 60–19,000 Hz. Thus, the microphone and speaker do not faithfully reproduce the lower pitched cardiac tones whose frequencies are 30–300 Hz.

Exercise 18   **Collecting Urine from Newborn Rabbits**

An effective technique of obtaining daily urine samples aseptically from neonate and young rabbits by manual restraint and abdominal stroking has been described (Garvey and Aalseth, 1971). The procedure is

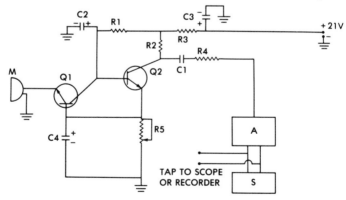

Figure 36. Schematic diagram of cardiac monitor. Transistors: Q_1, $Q_2$2N930. Capacitors: C_1—0.1 mfd, 50V, disk; C_2—4.7 mfd, 25V, elec.; C_3—50 mfd, 35V, elec.; and $C_4$50 mfd, 6V, elec. Resistors: R_1—20K; R_2—15K; R_3—1.8K; $R_4$1K; and R_5—1K. Microphone: M-carbon type (Radio Shack, Tandy Corp., Fort Worth, Texas, Cat. No. 270-095). Speaker: Four-inch acoustic suspension. Amplifier: Model AA-18 (Heathkit, Benton Harbor, Michigan).

noninvasive and allows urine collection from the 12-hour- to the 10-day-old rabbit. With simple modification of procedure, collections can be continued through the time of weaning and beyond.

Cradle the rabbit on its back with its head toward the wrist in your left hand. Press your left thumb down on the animal's left hind foot. Position your fingers so as to grip the rabbit firmly. With slight pressure gently stroke the rabbit's abdomen, using the thumb of your right hand. Extend the stroke from the level of the stomach caudally to just beyond the region of the bladder, moderately increasing the pressure at the bladder level.

Maintain stroking until urine is expressed as a continuous flow, releasing the pressure when the flow ceases. About 5 ml of urine can be obtained.

In a modification usually necessary after the tenth day, gently hold the rabbit around the neck and rib cage, using your thumb and little finger, allowing the hind limbs to be unrestrained. Since the animal has increased capacity to keep the vesical sphincters closed, use somewhat greater caudally directed manual pressure to release the bladder urine. The animal will require several hours for its bladder to refill. Under no circumstances exert a pressure that can produce internal injury or restriction of breathing.

Exercise 19 **Drawing Blood from the Orbital Sinus**

Use heparinized microhematocrit capillary tubes (75 mm long by 1.3 or 1.4 mm O.D.). Break off one end to reduce the length to 50 mm. Do not attempt to smooth the rough cutting edge. Sterilize the tubes.

With the rabbit restrained by an assistant, and held on its side with all limbs fully extended, hold the rabbit's head firmly with one hand and partially retract the eyelids with your thumb and forefinger.

Place the tip of the capillary tube in the dorsal junction of the bulbar and palpebral conjunctivas midway between the medial and lateral canthi of the eyes. Direct the long axis of the capillary tube somewhat ventrally and caudally in relation to the skull.

Penetrate the fibrous conjunctiva by thrusting the tube inward while rotating it between the thumb and the forefinger. The tube enters the venous sinus which is at or behind the equatorial region of the eyeball adjacent to the bony orbit. To obtain an adequate blood flow into the tube, seek optimal effects of gravity and venous pressure by turning the rabbit's head such that the outer end of the capillary tube is lowered. Remove the tube and apply digital pressure over the eyelid to stop blood flow. If clotting occurs during the procedure, repeat the steps in the other eye. In properly anticoagulated tubes, 5 ml of blood can be collected in 15–30 seconds.

Insert the capillary through a middorsal route and not through the medial or lateral canthus of the eye. Be aware of the possibilities of infection or of accidental trauma. It is not necessary to use a topical anesthetic.

Refer to Lumsden *et al.* (1974) for adaptation of the orbital sinus procedure to rabbits.

Exercise 20   **Lymphography**

Lymphography allows the study of lymphatic anatomy and physiology in the living animal, and it can be directed to pharmacologic, diagnostic, and therapeutic purposes. The procedure involves the injection of contrast media followed by visualization by radiography. The contrast medium can be injected directly into a lymphatic trunk or node or else into the tissues whence it is collected into the trunks or nodes.

Sedate the rabbit with 0.25 ml kilogram body weight of Innovar-Vet (Pitman-Moore, Fort Washington, Pennsylvania) injected intramuscularly or else produce general anesthesia with inhalant or injected drugs. Lymphography is performed in different body regions. For the lower trunk inject into the web space between the toes of the hind foot 11% Patent Blue Violet. This is transported in the superficial lymph vessels which are seen through the skin of the leg. Make a 2-cm skin incision adjacent to a lymph trunk on the medial aspect of the distal hindleg. Milk the blue dye up the lymph trunks making the trunks visible. A lymph trunk node visible as above can be exposed and punctured with a No. 27 or smaller needle attached to a syringe. Tie the needle in place with a No. 4–0 silk ligature previously placed around the visible lymph trunk. To visualize definitively for radiography the lymph vessels of the leg and popliteal nodes, use 1–2 ml of contrast material. The media are water-soluble organic iodides (e.g., Hypaque, Winthrop Laboratories, New York, New York) or colloidal or oily material (e.g., Ethiodol, E. Fougers & Co., Hicksville, New York). The former are lost quickly from the lymph so that radiographs must be made immediately.

The initial injection of Patent Blue Violet was to allow identification of the lymph vessels. With operator experience this step may be eliminated. Squeezing the animal's paw will pump lymph into a trunk and the distention aids recognition.

Subcutaneous injection of blue dye elsewhere shows the position of lymphatics in those areas and facilitates injection. The approximate site for skin incision in a white rabbit is revealed by fine blue streaks radiating from the area of injection. Massaging the region containing the dye helps detect a larger vessel with which to work.

It is feasible to directly inject the contrast medium for radiography into a lymph node. In working in the leg region incise over the popliteal fossa. Squeeze together the medial and lateral surfaces to deliver the popliteal node into the wound. Inject medium into the node slowly with a No. 27 needle.

In long-term studies use aseptic technique, and close a wound, following hemostasis and saline irrigation, with fine silk or catgut. Use bandaging and antibiotics.

For radiography any standard x-ray apparatus is satisfactory. Obtain dorsoventral and lateral view films. Since contrast medium flow is slow in the lymphatics, rapid cassette changes and cinefluorography are usually unnecessary.

In the technique of microlymphangiography, use either water-soluble or colloidal contrast medium. Inject the substance into the subcutaneous tissue of the ear or leg of the rabbit through a No. 18 needle.

References

Allen, W. F. (1931). An experimentally produced premature systolic arrhythmia, pulsus bigeminus, in rabbits. *Am. J. Physiol.* **98**, 334–351.

Altman, P. E., and Dittmer, D.S., eds. (1972). "Biology Data Book," 2nd ed., Vol. 1. Fed. Am. Soc. Exp. Biol., Baltimore Maryland.

Banta, C. A., Banta, R. G., Belin, R. P., and Wekstein, D. R. A. (1972). Low-cost cardiac auscultation device for monitoring rabbits under general anesthesia. *Lab. Anim. Sci.* **22**, 402–403.

Bieter, R. N., Cunningham, R. W., Lenz, O., and McNearny, J. J. (1936). Threshold anesthetic and lethal concentrations of certain spinal anesthetics in the rabbit. *J. Pharmacol. Exp. Ther.* **57**, 221–244.

Blume, G. F., and Fang, K. (1937). Effects of parathyroid hormone on platelet count and coagulation time of blood. *Chin J. Physiol.* **11**, 103–106.

Boegli, R. G., and Hall, I. H. (1969). A surgical external biliary fistula for the total collection of bile from rabbits. *Lab. Anim. Care* **19**, 657–658.

Bredderman, R. H., Foote, R. H., and Yassen, A. M., (1964). An improved artificial vagina for collecting rabbit semen. *J. Reprod. Fertil.* **7**, 401–403.

Bree, M. M., and Cohen, B. J. (1965). Effects of urethane anesthesia on blood and vessels in rabbits. *Lab. Anim. Care* **15**, 254–259.

Burke, J. C., (1977). Blood collecting by the ear artery method. *Lab. Anim.* **11**, 49.

Courtice, F. C., and Gunton, R. W. (1949). The determination of blood volume by carbon monoxide and dye (T–1824) methods in rabbits. *J. Physiol.*, **108**, 405–417.

Castor, G. B., and Zaldivar, R. A. (1973). Tattooing rabbits' ears for identification. *Lab. Anim. Sci.* **23**, 279–281.

David, A., Czernobilisky, B., and Kaplun, A. (1974). A new technical approach for the study of endometrium regeneration in the rabbit. *Lab. Anim. Sci.* **24**, 552–557.

Davis, R. H., McDonald J. F., Kyriazis, G. A., and Schneider, H. P. (1974). The peritoneal fluid cellular content of adult female New Zealand white rabbits. *Lab. Anim. Sci.* **24**, 101–102.

Decker, S. E., and Heller, E. (1945). The mechanism of water diuresis in normal rats and rabbits as analyzed by inulin and diodone clearance. *J. Physiol. (London)* **103**, 449–460.

Dolowy, W. C., and Hesse, A. L. (1959). Chlorpromazine premedication with pentobarbital anesthesia in the rabbit. *J. Am. Vet. Med. Assoc.* **134**, 183–184.

Downman, C. B. B., MacKenzie, C. C., and McSwiney, B. A. (1944). The effects of acute hemorrhage on the peripheral blood pressure in unanesthetized and in anesthetized rabbits. *J. Physiol. (London)* **103**, 350–357.

Dudley, W. R., Soma, L. R., Barnes, C., Smith, T. C., and Marshall, B. E. (1975). An apparatus for anesthetizing small laboratory animals. *Lab. Anim. Sci.* **25**, 481–482.

Elchlepp, J. G. (1952). The urogenital organs of the cottontail rabbit *(Sylvilagus floridanus)*. *J. Morphol.* **91**, 169–198.

Fee, A. R., and Parkes, A. S. (1929). Studies on ovulation. I. The relation of the anterior pituitary body to ovulation in the rabbit. *J. Physiol.* **87**, 383–388.

Firor, W. M. (1933). Hypophysectomy in pregnant rabbits. *Am. J. Physiol.* **104**, 204–15.

Firor, W. M., and Grollman, A. (1933). Adrenalectomy in mammals with particular reference to the white rat, *Mus norvegicus. Am. J. Physiol.* **103**, 686–698.

Fox, R. R., and Crary, D. D. (1972). A simple technique for the sexing of newborn rabbits. *Lab. Anim. Sci.* **22**, 556–558.

Gardner, A. F. (1964). The development of general anesthesia in the albino rabbit for surgical procedures. *Lab. Anim Care* **14**, 214–225.

Garvey, J. S., and Aalseth, B. L. (1971). Urine collection from newborn rabbits. *Lab. Anim. Sci.* **21**, 739.

Glass, R. H. (1972). Fate of rabbit eggs fertilized in the uterus. *J. Reprod. Fertil.* **31**, 139–141.

Hafez, E. S. E. (1961). Storage of rabbit ova in gelled media at 10°C. *J. Reprod. Fertil.* **2**, 163–178.

Hafez, E. S. E. (1970). "Rabbits. Reproduction and Breeding Techniques for Laboratory Animals." Lea & Febiger, Philadelphia, Pennsylvania.

Hall, L. L., DeLopez, O. H., Roberts, A., and Smith, F. A. (1974). A procedure for chronic intravenous catheterization in the rabbit. *Lab. Anim. Sci.* **24**, 79–83.

Hodesson, S., Rich, S. T., Washington, J. O., and Apt, L. (1965). Anesthesia of the rabbit with Equi-Thesin following administration of preanesthetics. *Lab. Anim. Care* **15**, 336–344.

Hoge, R. S., Hodesson, S., Snow, I. B., and Wood, A. I. (1969). Intubation technique and methoxyflurane administration in rabbits. *Lab. Anim. Care* **19**, 593–595.

Jacobs, H. R. (1937). Hypoglycemic action of alloxan. *Proc. Soc. Exp. Biol. Med.* **37**, 407–409.

Kaplan, B. I., and Smith, H. W. (1935). Excretion of inulin, creatinine, xylose and urea in the normal rabbit. *Am. J. Physiol.* **113**, 354–360.

Kennelly, J. J., and Foote, R. H. (1965). Superovulatory response to pre-and post-pubertal rabbits to commercially available gonadotrophins. *J. Reprod. Fertil.* **9**, 176–188.

Kracke, R. (1947). "Color Atlas of Hematology." Lippincott, Philadelphia, Pennsylvania.

Lang, C. M. (1976). "Animal Physiologic Surgery." Springer-Verlag, Berlin and New York.

Lindquist, P. A. (1972). Induction of methoxyflurane anesthesia in the rabbit after Ketamine hydrochloride and endo-tracheal intubation. *Lab. Anim. Sci.* **22**, 898–899.

Lumb, W. V., and Jones, E. W. (1973). "Veterinary Anesthesia." Lea & Febiger, Philadelphia, Pennsylvania.

Lumsden, J. H., Presidente, P. J. A., and Quinn, P. J. (1974). Modification of the orbital sinus bleeding technic for rabbits. *Lab. Anim. Sci.* **24**, 345–348.

McCormick, N. J., and Ashworth, M. A. (1971). Acepromazine and methoxyflurane anesthesia of immature New Zealand white rabbits. *Lab. Anim. Sci.* **21**, 220–223.

McGregor, L. (1928). A new indirect method for taking blood pressure in animals. *Arch. Pathol.* **5**, 630–660.

"Manual of Operative Procedure and Surgical Knots." (1968). Ethicon, Inc., Somerville, New Jersey.

Martin, W. J., and Marcus, S. (1964). Studies on bacterial pyrogenicity. *Appl. Microbiol.* **12**, 483–486.

Mayer, K., Lacroix, J. V., and Hoskins, H. P. (1957). "Canine Surgery," 4th ed. Am. Vet. Publ., Inc., Santa Barbara, California.

Moir, A. T. B., and Dow, R. C. (1970). A simple method allowing perfusion of cerebral ventricles of the conscious rabbit: cerebrospinal fluid. *J. Appl. Physiol.* 28, 528–529.

Nice, L. B., and Katz, H. L. (1936). Emotional leucopenia in rabbits. *Am. J. Physiol.* 117, 571–575.

Pakes, S. P., Shadduck J. A., and Olsen, R. G. (1972). A diagnostic skin test for encephalito-zoonosis (nosematosis) in rabbits. *Lab. Anim. Sci.* 22, 870–877.

Papanicolaou, G. (1932). "Atlas of Exfoliative Cytology." Harvard Univ. Press, Cambridge, Massachusetts.

Powsner, E. R., and Fly, M. N. (1962). Aseptic aspiration of bone marrow from the living rabbit. *J. Appl. Physiol.* 17, 1021–1022.

Sawin, P. B., Green, E. L., and Johnson, R. B. (1938). Sexing newborn rabbits. *J. Mammal.* 19, 109–110.

Skartvedt, S. M., and Lyon, N. C. (1972). A simple apparatus for inducing and maintaining halothane anesthesia of the rabbit. *Lab. Anim. Sci.* 22, 922–924.

Smith, P. E., and White, W. E. (1931). The effect of hypophysectomy on ovulation and corpus luteum formation in the rabbit. *J. Am. Med. Assoc.* 97, 1861–1863.

Strack, L. E., and Kaplan, H. M. (1968). Fentanyl and droperidol for surgical anesthesia of rabbits. *J. Am. Vet. Med. Assoc.* 153, 822–825.

Tatum, A. L. (1913). Morphological studies in experimental cretinism. *J. Exp. Med.* 17, 636–652.

U.S. National Institutes of Health (1969). Div. Biol. Stand., "Biologic Products." USNIH, Bethesda, Maryland.

U.S. Pharmacopeia (1970). "Pyrogen Test," 18th ed., pp. 886–887. Mack Printing Co., Easton, Pennsylvania.

Walton, A. (1958) Improvement in the design of an artificial vagina for the rabbit. *J. Physiol. (London)* 143, 26P–28P.

Wass, J., Keene, J., and Kaplan, H.M. (1974). Ketamine-methoxyflurane anesthesia for rabbits. *Am. J. Vet. Res.* 352, 317–318.

Watson, S.C., and Cowie, A.T. (1966). A simple closed-circuit apparatus for cyclopropane and halothane anesthesia for the rabbit. *Lab. Anim. Care* 166, 515–519.

Weary, M.E., Wallin, R.F. (1973). The rabbit pyrogen test. *Lab. Anim. Sci.* 23, 677–681.

Weisbroth, S.H., and Fudens, J.H. (1972). Use of ketamine hydrochloride as an anesthetic in laboratory rabbits, rats, mice and guinea pigs. *Lab. Anim. Sci.* 22, 904–906.

Weisbroth, S.H., Flatt, R.E., and Kraus, A.L., eds. (1974). "Biology of the the Laboratory Rabbit." Academic Press, New York.

Wilburne, M., Schlichter, J.G., Grossman, M., and Cisneros, F. (1947). The use of acetylcholine in the objective determination of circulation time and the fractionation of the vascular bed traversed. *Am. J. Physiol.* 150, 504–510.

Wintrobe, M.M., Shumacker, H.B., and Schmidt, W.J. (1936). Values for number, size and hemoglobin content of erythrocytes in normal dogs, rabbits and rats, *Am. J. Physiol.* 114, 502–507.

Suggested Reading

Altman, P. E., and Dittmer, D. S., eds. (1971) "Respiration and Circulation." Fed. Am. Soc. Exp. Biol., Baltimore, Maryland.

Altman, P. E., and Dittmer, D. S., eds. (1972), (1973), (1974). "Biology Data Book," 2nd ed., Vols. 1,2,3, Fed. Am. Soc. Exp. Biol., Baltimore, Maryland.

Arrington, L. R., and Kelley, K. C. (1977) "Domestic Rabbit Biology and Production." University Presses of Florida, Gainesville.

"Bibliography of Agriculture." National Agricultural Library, U. S. Department of Agriculture, Washington, D. C. (issued monthly, see Contents: Rabbits). (1974).

Brown, H. (1974). "Protein Nutrition." Thomas, Springfield, Illinois.

Cole, W. H., and Zollinger, R. M., eds. (1970). "Textbook of Surgery," 9th ed. Appleton, New York.

Coles, E. H. (1974). "Veterinary Clinical Pathology," 2nd ed. Saunders, Philadelphia, Pennsylvania.

Ethicon, (1968). "Manual of Operative Procedure and Surgical Knots." Ethicon, Inc., Somerville, New Jersery.

Evans, G. E., and Thomson, D. (1972). "The Leaping Hare." Faber & Faber, London.

Graham-Jones, O., ed. (1964). "Small Animal Anaesthesia." Macmillan, New York.

Hall, L. W. (1971) "Wright's Veterinary Anaesthesia and Analgesia," 7th ed., Baillière, London.

Harkness, J. E., and Wagner, J. E. (1977). "The Biology and Medicine of Rabbits and Rodents." Lea & Febiger, Philadelphia, Pennsylvania.

Institute of Laboratory Animal Resources (1972). "Guide for the Care and Use of Laboratory Animals," DHEW Publ. No. (NIH) 74–23. ILAR (NAS-NRC), Washington, D. C.

Lane-Petter, W., Worden, A. N., Hill, F. B., Paterson, J. S., and Vevers, H. G. (1976). "The UFAW Handbook on the Care and Management of Laboratory Animals," 5th ed. UFAW, London.

Lang, C. M. (1976). "Animal Physiologic Surgery." Springer-Verlag, Berlin and New York.

Lumb, W. V., and Jones, E. W. (1973). "Veterinary Anesthesia." Lea & Febiger, Philadelphia, Pennsylvania.

Markowitz, J., Archibald, J., and Downie, H. G. (1964). "Experimental Surgery," 5th ed. Williams & Wilkins, Baltimore, Maryland.

Mayer, K., Lacroix, J. V., and Hoskins, H. P. (1957). "Canine Surgery," 4th ed. Am. Vet. Publ., Inc., Santa Barbara, California.

Menaker, L., ed. (1975). "Biologic Basis of Wound Healing." Harper, New York.

Siegmund, O. H., ed. (1973). "The Merck Veterinary Manual," 4th ed. Merck and Company, Rahway, New Jersey.

Weisbroth, S. H., Flatt, R. E., and Kraus, A. L., eds. (1974). "Biology of the Laboratory Rabbit." Academic Press, New York.

Westhues, M., and Fritsch, R. (1964). "Animal Anesthesia." Lippincott, Philadelphia, Pennsylvania.

Subject Index